F E R I T   K U Y A S

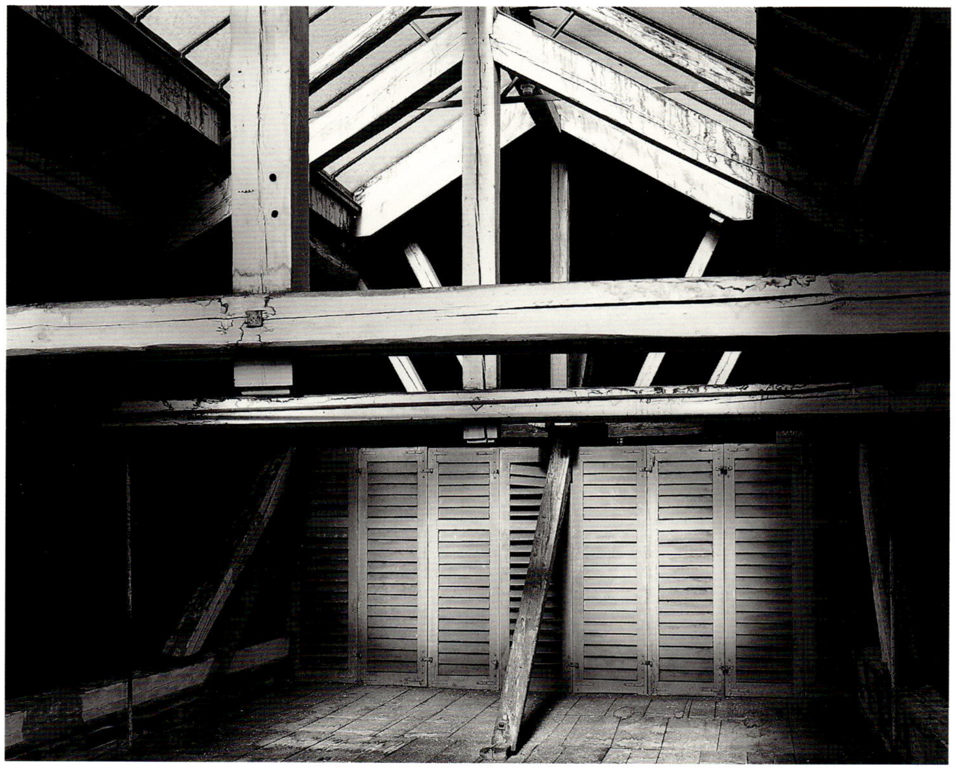

FERIT KUYAS

INDUSTRIAL INTERIORS

Texts by Hans-Peter Bärtschi, Benedikt Loderer and Ferit Kuyas

EDITION STEMMLE

Zurich New York

To My Parents

Contents

6

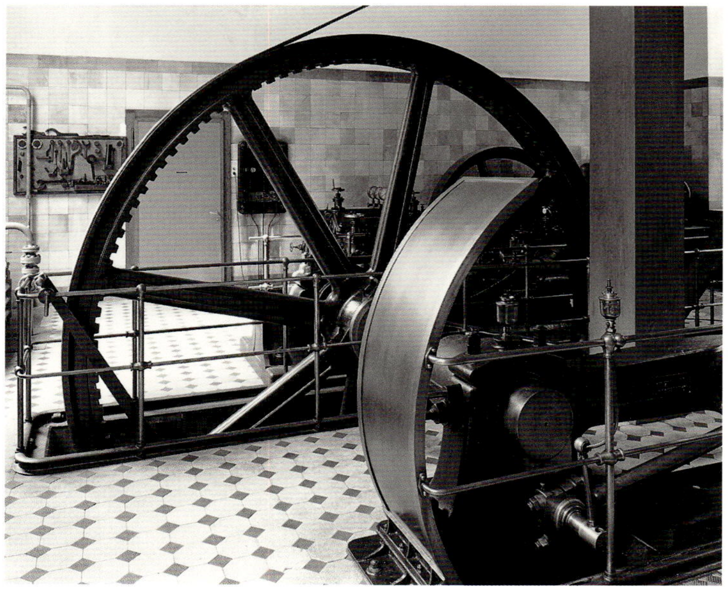

Foreword

Hans-Peter Bärtschi

Over a period of eight years, from 1988 to 1995, Ferit Kuyas focused his creative camera on industrial interiors. These were the years when recession in Switzerland led to "deindustrialization" on an unprecedented scale. Until 1966 her unemployment rate had been vastly below that of other industrialized nations such as Great Britain or Belgium. Then the industrial labor force was halved within two decades—which not only took unemployment in Switzerland to its highest level since the 1930s, but put 400 square kilometers of industrial plant and office facilities out of action. Familiar workaday scenes were suddenly frozen; factories were shut down, demolished or reutilized. Disconsolately contemplating those derelict sites, clinging aimlessly to lifeless piping and redundant railings, we blindly surveyed the vestiges of bygone labors and failed to see the hidden allure of majestic machinery and industrial settings. But Ferit Kuyas has the vision we lacked: he has vividly recorded these everyday scenes for posterity. With infinite patience he has made optimal use of natural lighting effects, carrying heavy large-format equipment with him wherever he went. He has invested countless hours in photographing, developing and enlarging. And his unerring eye reveals aspects otherwise lost to our gaze—the pictures invite us to forget our absurdly hectic times and rediscover the massive durability of industrial interiors going back 50, 100 or 170 years.

Ferit Kuyas' industrial interiors show the texture in light and shadow of power stations, spinning mills, machine works and breweries. Many of the subjects were chosen with a view to selected publications and exhibitions. The intensive study of spinning mills, for example, was completed by 1994 for exhibitions in Uster and Neuthal and for the fifteenth jubilee edition of "Der Industrielehrpfad Zürcher Oberland" (On the Trail of Industrial History in the Zurich Uplands).
On the other hand, his purely idealistic motivation has led to a photographic documentation of Swiss power stations, the disused mines in Goppenstein and the Feldschlösschen brewery, and of the old Basle incineration plant which was demolished immediately afterwards. This book thus shows not only what has been found worthy of preservation, but in particular it records for posterity some outstanding examples of industrial archeology which have since been destroyed.

8

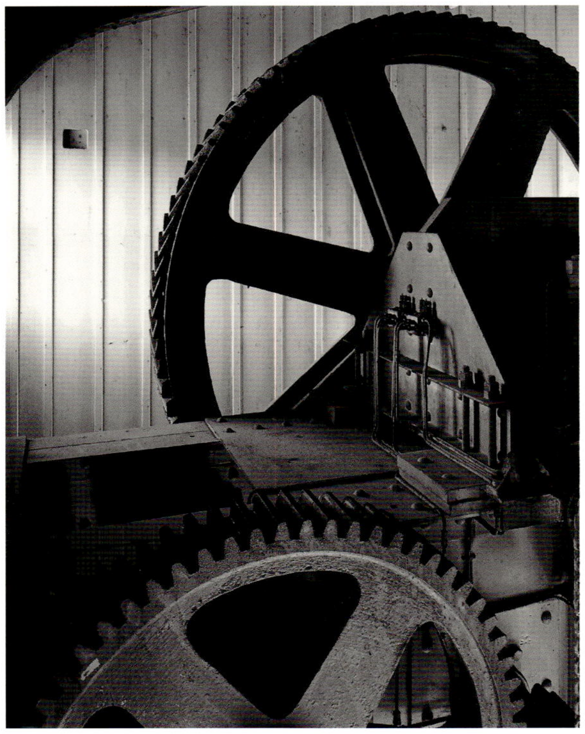

Power and Silence: Bearing Witness to the Past

Benedikt Loderer

We enter, we descend, we submerge ourselves—in a strange interior world of its own. Behind us, the locked and bolted door cuts off any chance of escape. Claustrophobic panic seizes us, but then we shrug it off and tell ourselves that after all, these are only pictures deliberately arranged, selectively framed—just photographs. They consist only of space, light and surface textures: the stuff of which the photographer makes his pictures. Nothing else. And we already feel relieved, for sober analysis is the only escape we have.

Why did we not realize this from the beginning, from our first glance at these pictures? Surely after seeing so many others before, our self-protective instinct should be second nature? But with Ferit Kuyas' works, we can no longer protect ourselves by resorting to superficiality—they are far too subtle. We are drawn relentlessly into these pictures by an irresistible force, rather like a whirlpool, whose deadly pull seems so harmless at first. Our cursory glance is riveted. How can this uncanny effect be explained? For me there are three reasons: their power, their silence, and the witness they bear to the past.

As in physics, we cannot fully comprehend the meaning of power, but we can observe and measure its effects. In the case of Ferit Kuyas, the main effect is that instead of merely looking at his pictures, we inevitably become immersed in them. He has spent so long observing his subjects in such depth, that we have no other option than to do the same. These photographs are charged with an energy which we feel without knowing how or why—and I suspect that Ferit Kuyas himself has the same experience. He loses himself in the subject matter of each picture, and he cannot escape until the camera has passed its verdict. Whatever task he undertakes, he is compelled to master it. It is this mastery which captures the nascent power in photographic form—which like a caged tiger, tugs at its fetters and tries to escape at the first opportunity. And as the tiger threatens to pounce, we are hypnotized and cannot avert our gaze.

In other words, we are captured by the captured. But how? The physicist cannot tell us the answer—and neither can the photographer. The secret remains unsolved, but the main thing is the effect, not the explanation.

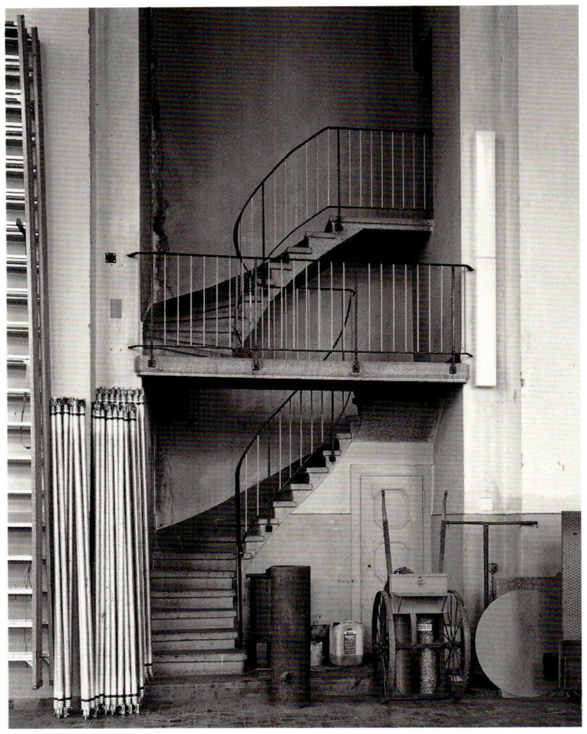

What about the silence of these pictures? It is the silence of abandonment. Formerly filled with bustle and noise, these industrial interiors are now empty and forsaken. Nothing happens any more. All activity has ceased. Time has been frozen and brought to a standstill. That is not to say that all the factories and workshops shown here are still lying derelict, but their essence of time has been caught in a photograph. And now at last we grasp the situation: these interiors have been transfixed and can no longer escape. In pictorial form, they can never again move or change. Even their decay has been halted: they are forced to obey the camera and keep their peace. Sleeping Beauty's castle? The magic sway of Ferit Kuyas is not merely for a hundred years—these gray-toned interiors will remain frozen for ever in a world of two dimensions.

As soon as we stop and look, we are alone. Just as it is for the photographer, the lone hunter, our world is suddenly devoid of companions. There is nobody to call our name, no one to search for us—in fact nobody even knows where we are. Because we are submerged in a sea of silence, disturbed only perhaps by the slamming of a door in the wind, or the rush of water in some subterranean canal. Neither we nor the photographer have any say in this world—we observe it through soundproof windows—curiously far away, it surrounds us nevertheless. And this world is devoid of echoes, because, as in a vacuum, we have no voice. It is penetrated with light, but no light escapes. For deep sea divers, the outside world does not exist.

And finally: the traces which bear witness to the past. Once, everything in this bygone world had a purpose. Each object had its designated use and necessity—and continues to speak the same language even now. But what used to be commonplace and workaday is now a difficult story to tell, even more difficult than the sweated labor of those times. For such stories always tell of loss and deprivation, of what has disappeared and no longer exists.

They also tell of burt force and sheer power, of steam and water, fire and molten metal, the grinding clash of machinery, enormous pressures and massive inertia, suffocating heat and freezing cold. Materials were swallowed by machines, battered into shape and regurgitated. And all this force, power and energy is engraved in the traces still evident here—wounds opened and reopened, scars inflamed by whole lifetimes of machinery. It is these traces that infuse Ferit Kuyas' pictures with their melancholic nostalgia of a last farewell, the fading moments of a bygone age. What we see today no longer exists. The traces have been erased and their stories have been told. Only Ferit Kuyas' camera has recorded them for posterity. Their day is done: the cause they stood for is no longer acclaimed.

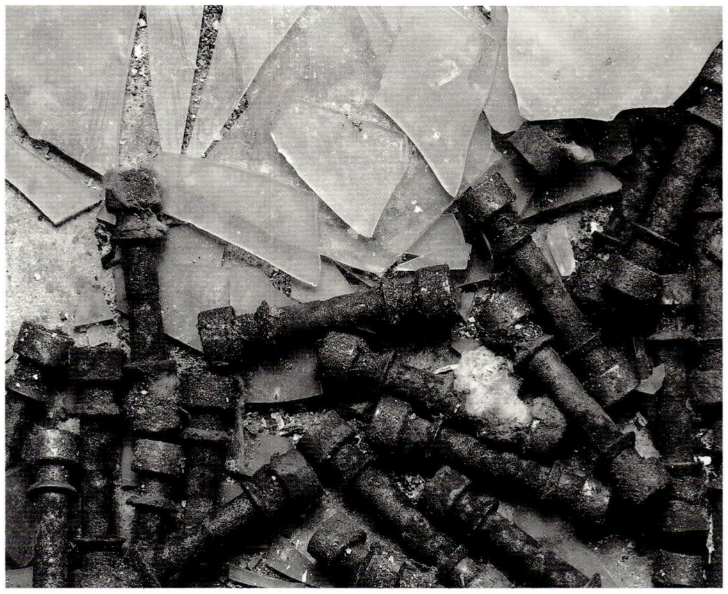

Now they are all just pictures. And it is as pictures that their new life begins. Ferit Kuyas has carried out this work as a self-imposed task, with uncompromising care and precision. I can see him now in his darkroom retreat. Totally engrossed and totally alone, he concentrates step by step on the finest nuances—the thin thread of patience must never be allowed to break. Each individual picture emerges in painstaking detail, methodically and unhurriedly. This photographer is the true successor to the master engravers of old: each step in his work is decisive. To Ferit Kuyas, the very mention of a snapshot is abhorrent.

And in the end, we are left with the result: a growing collection of works with enduring value. Each one of them radiating inexorable power as a silent witness to the past.

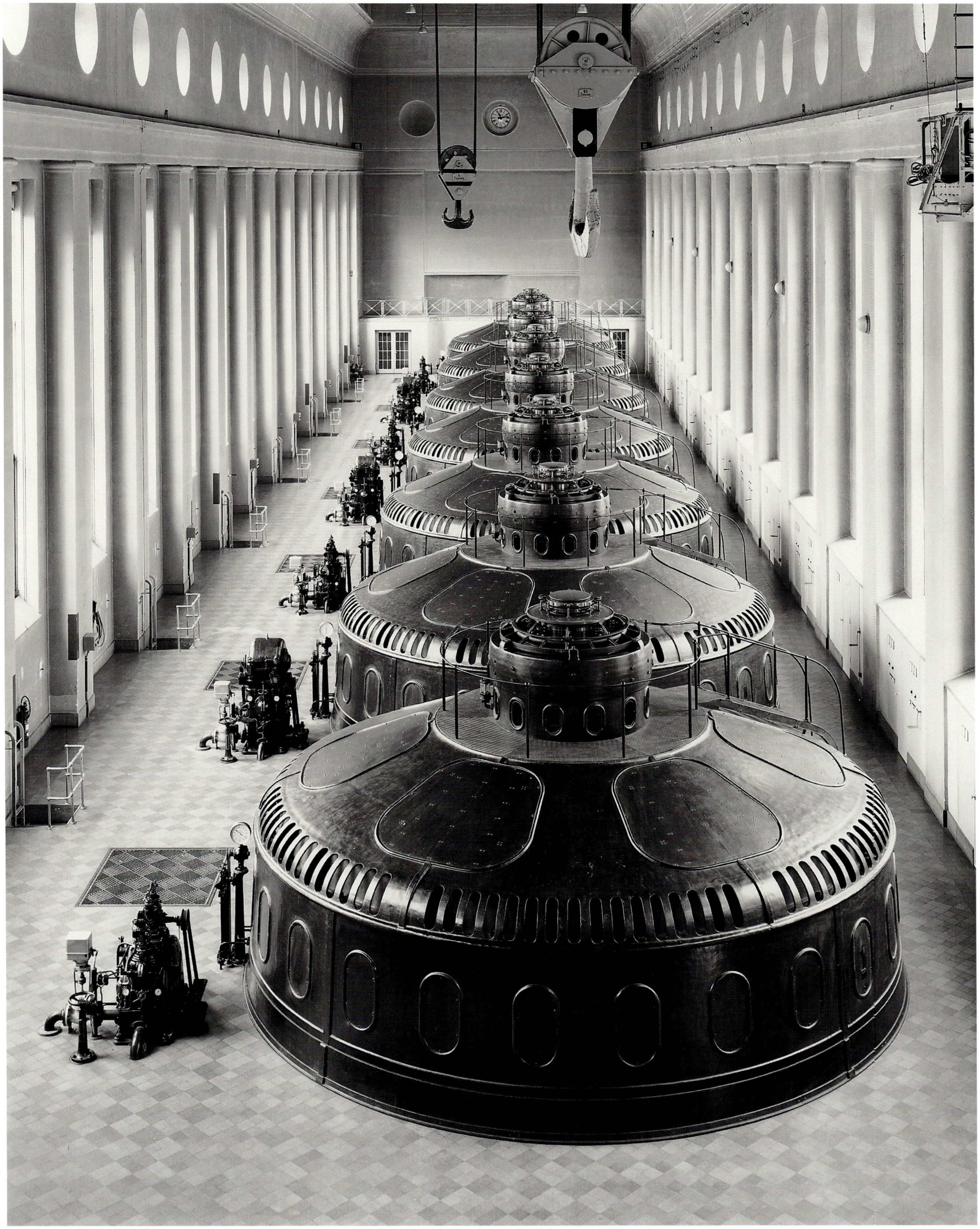

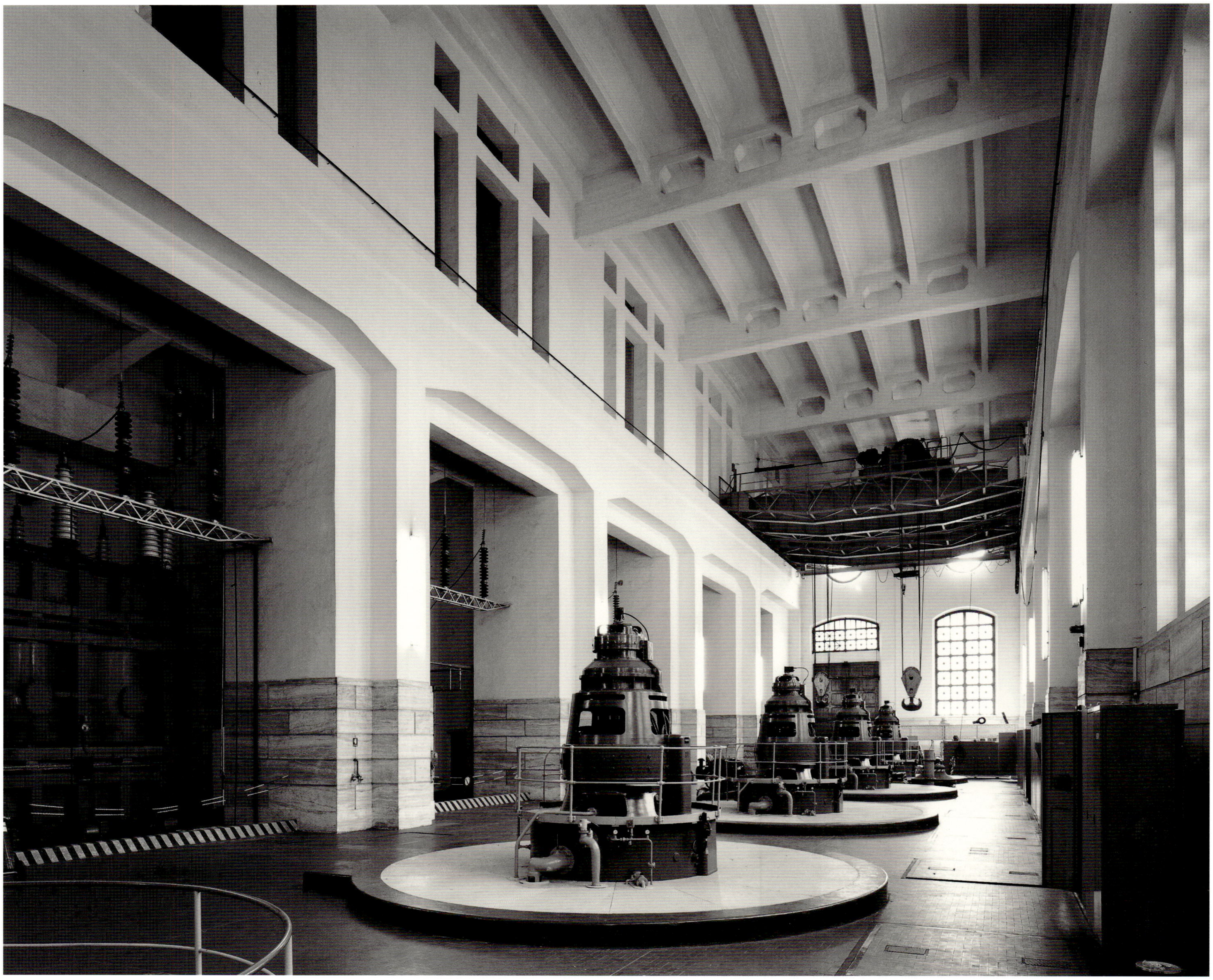

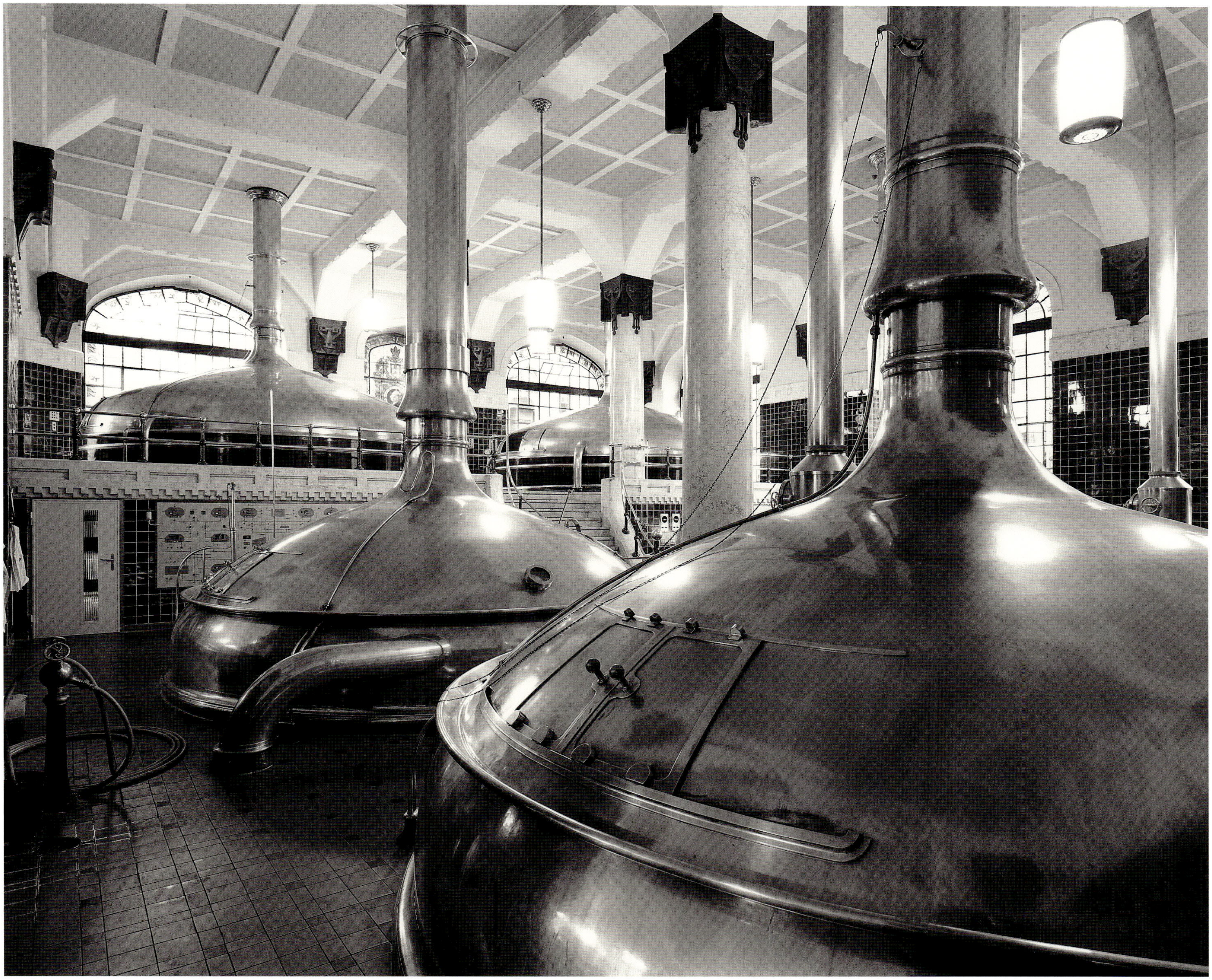

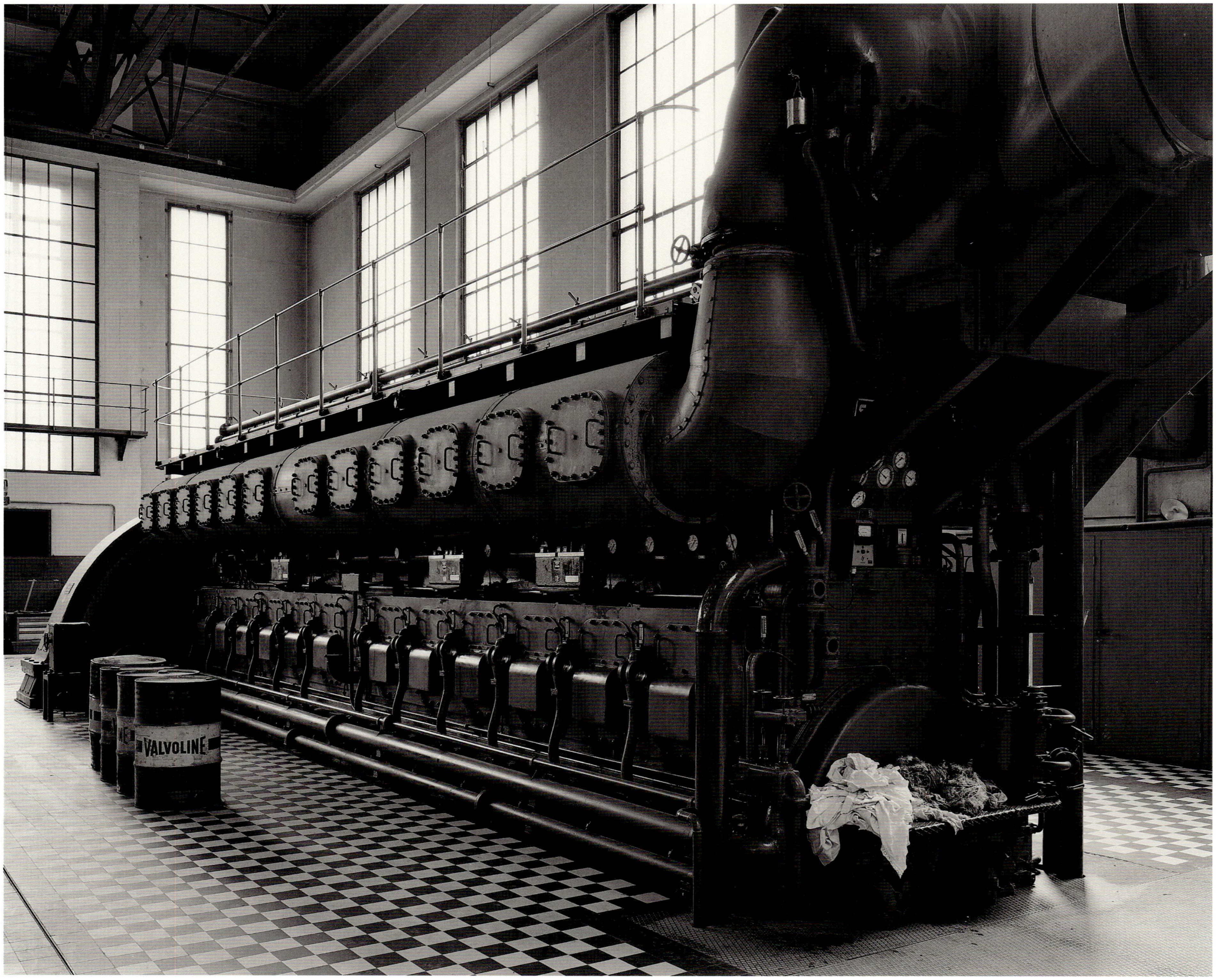
VALVOLINE

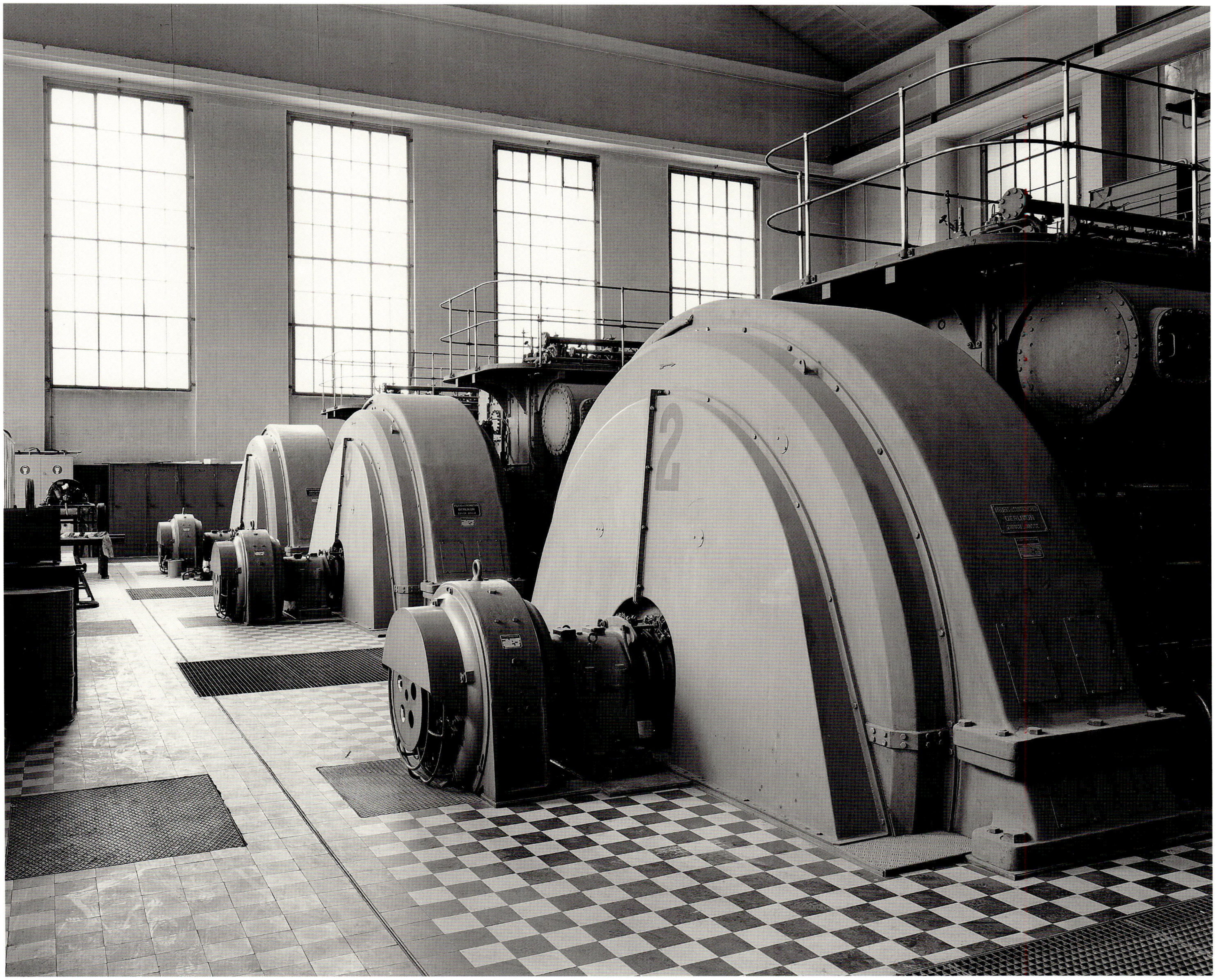
2

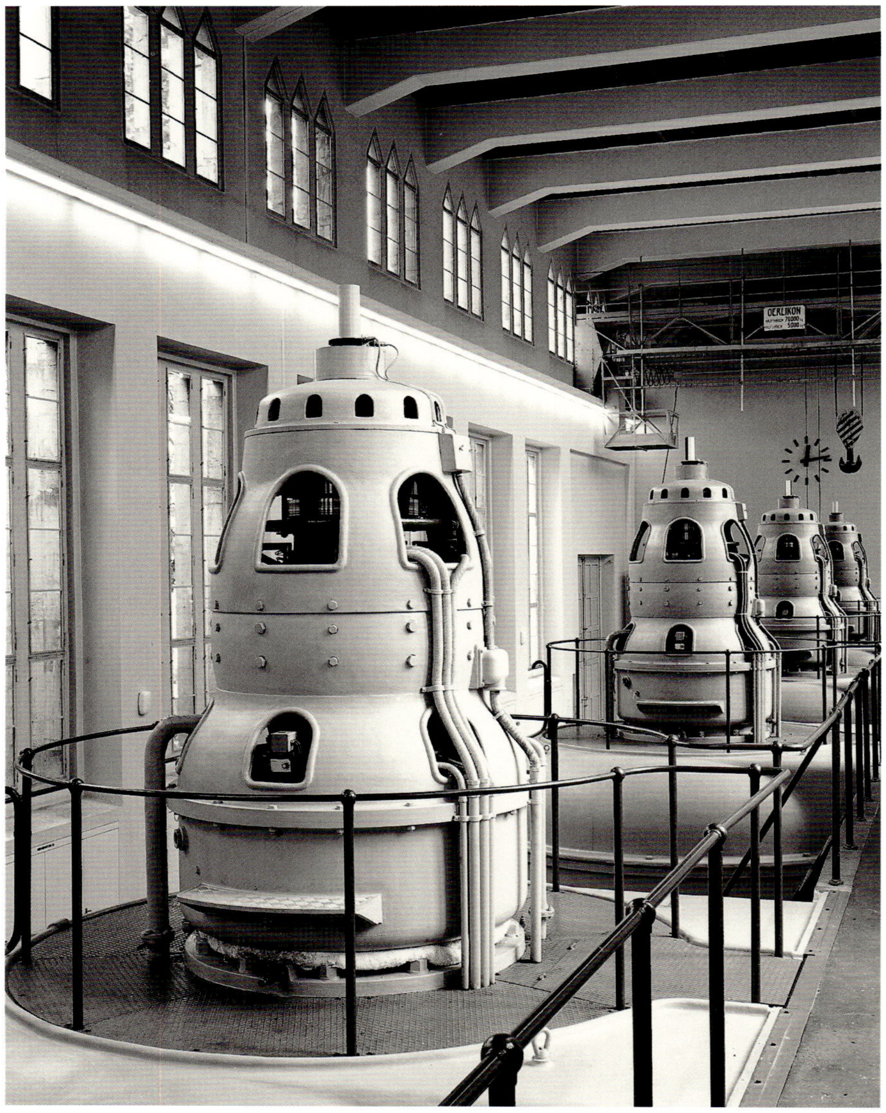
OERLIKON

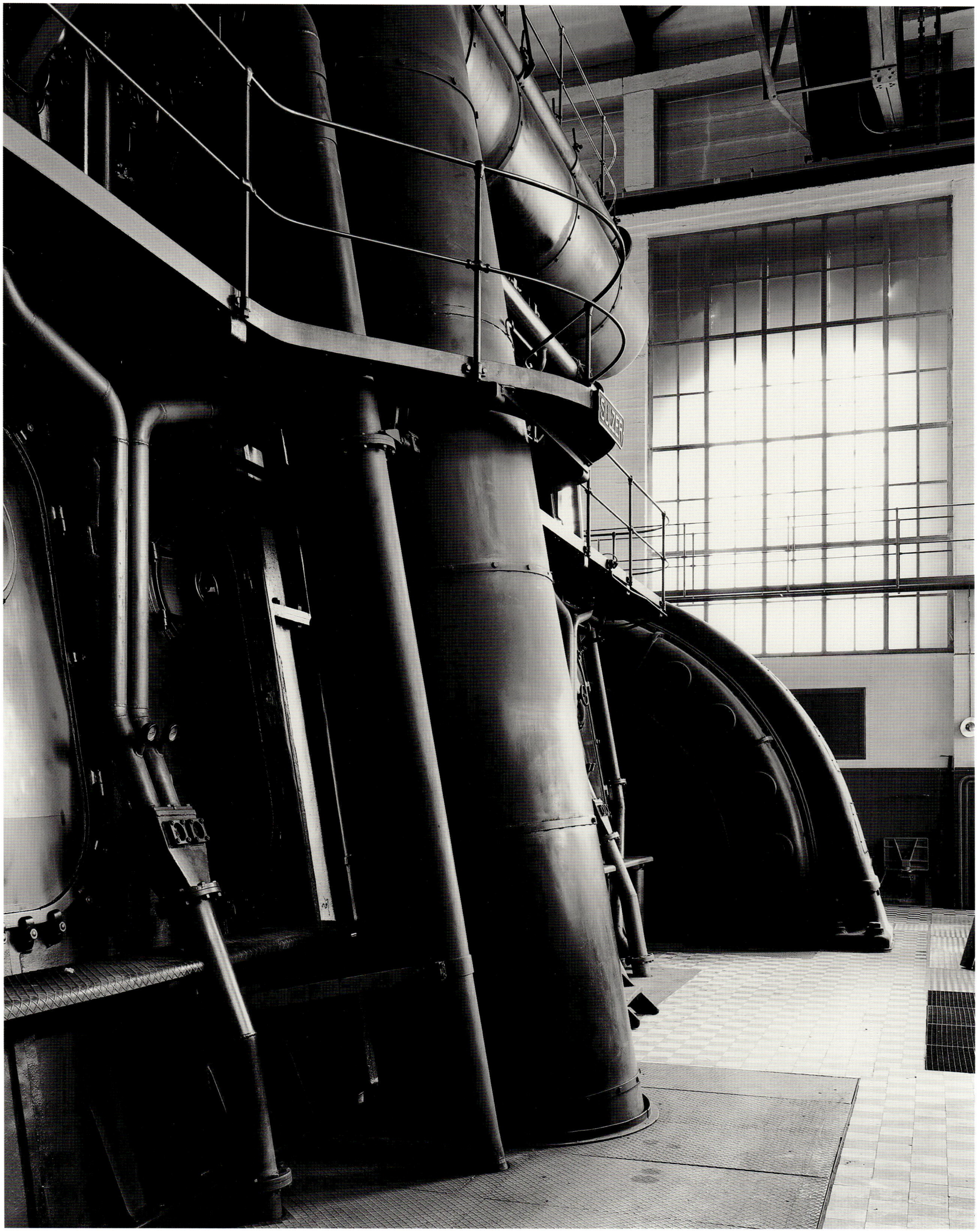
SULZER

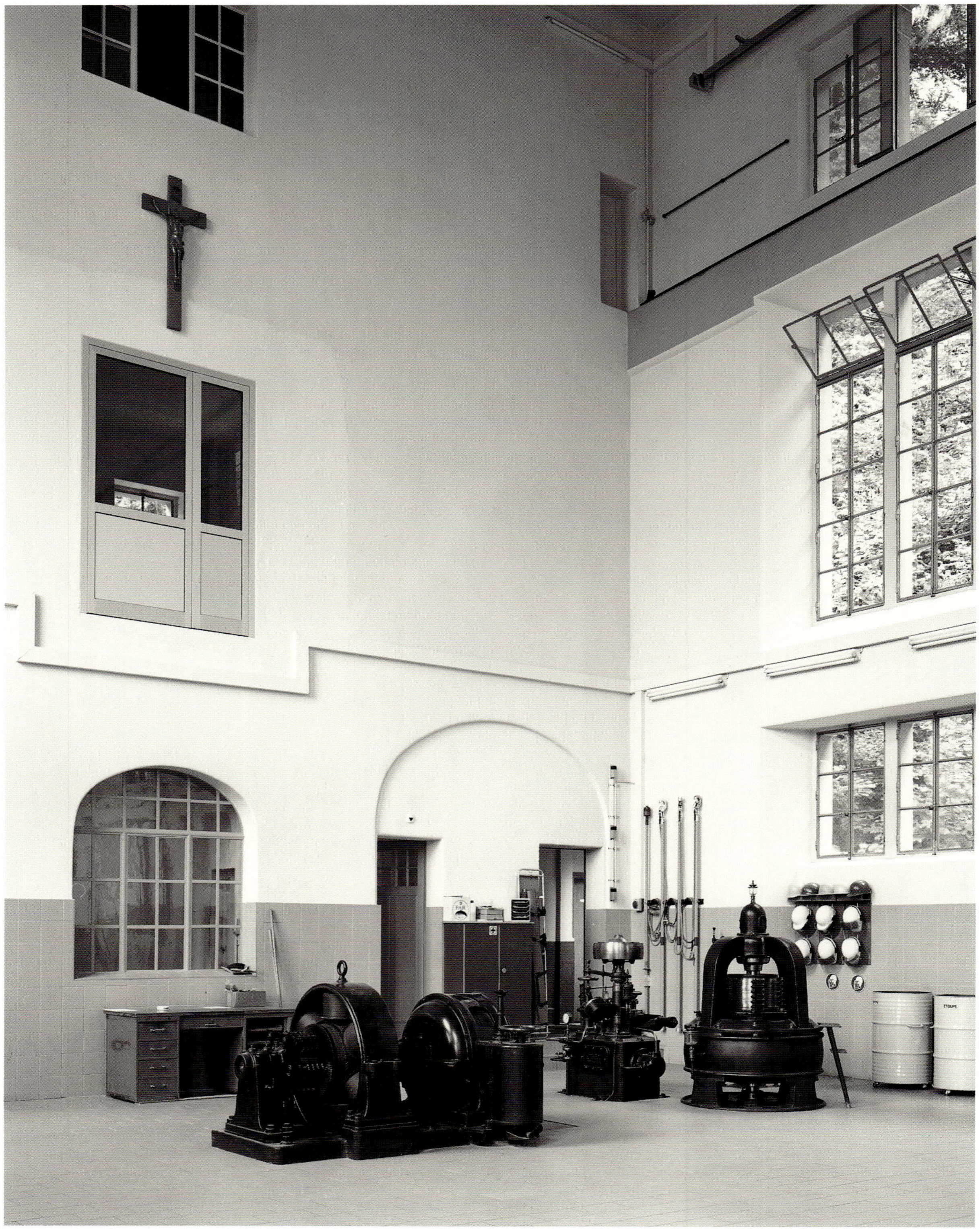

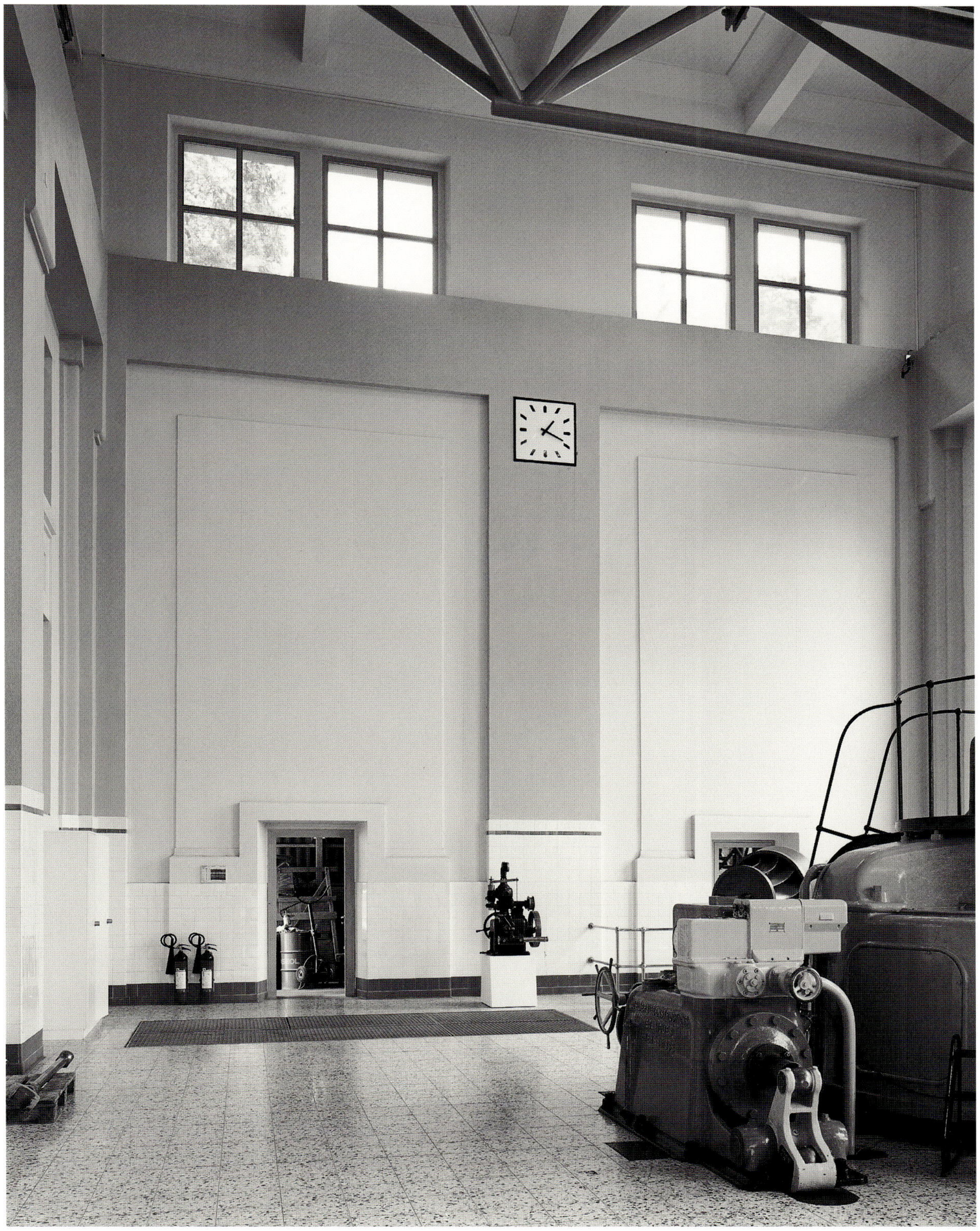

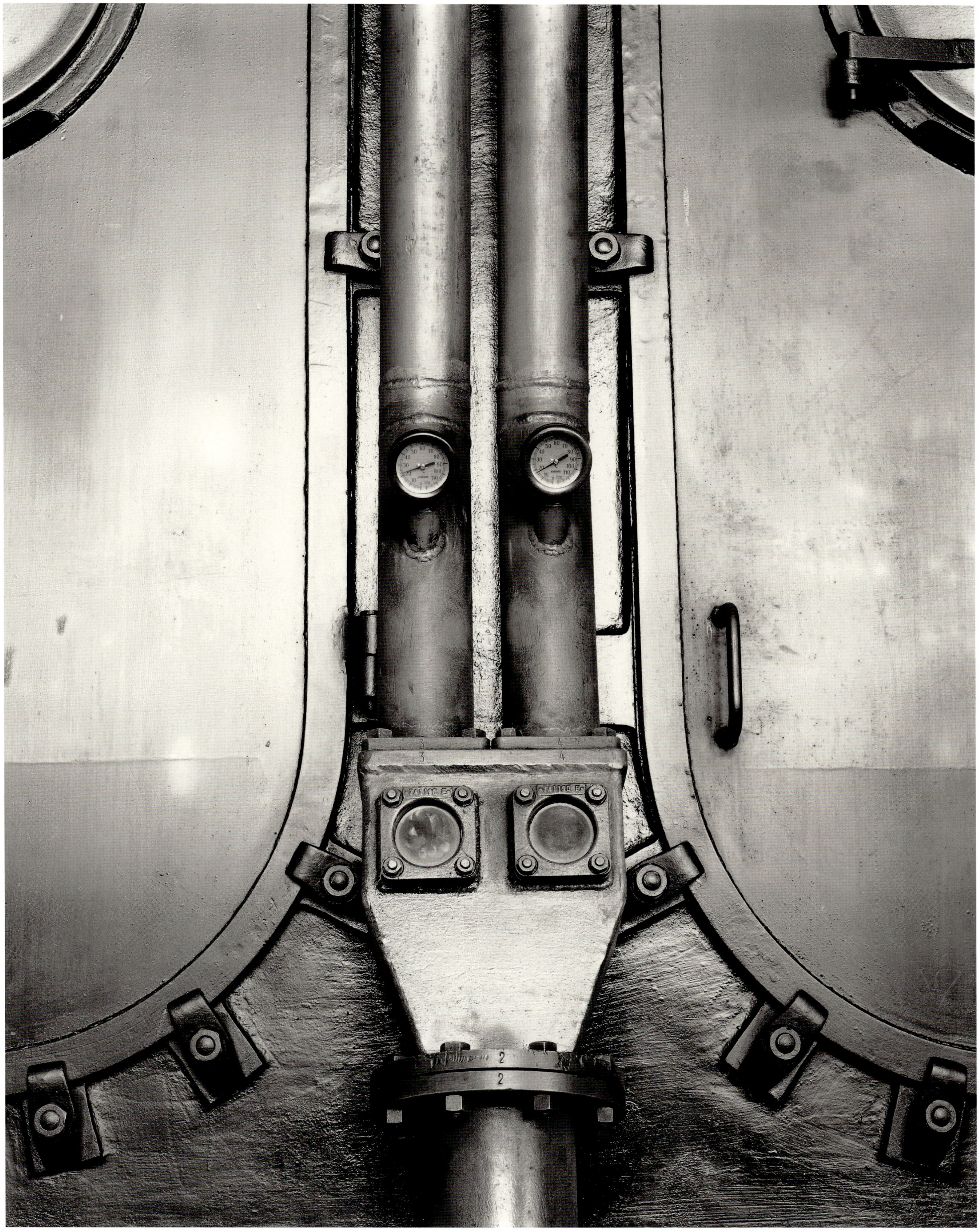

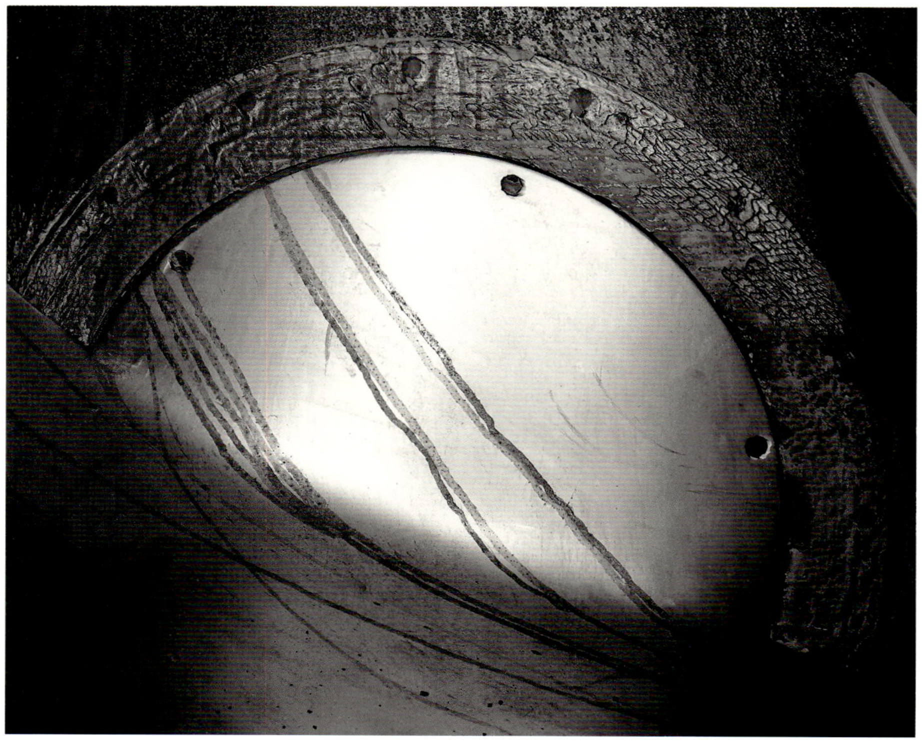

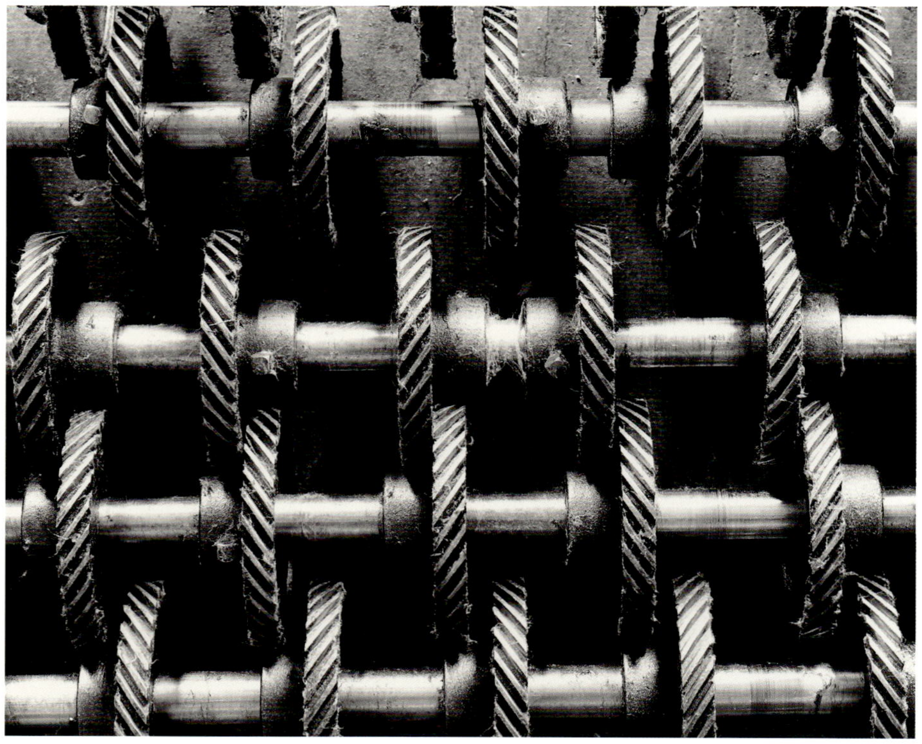

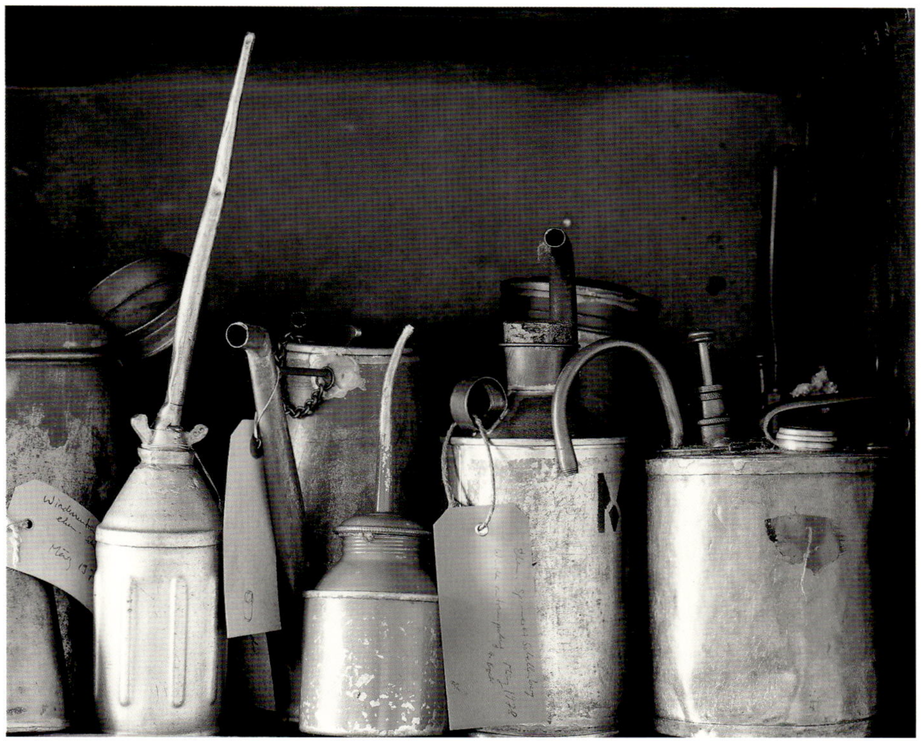

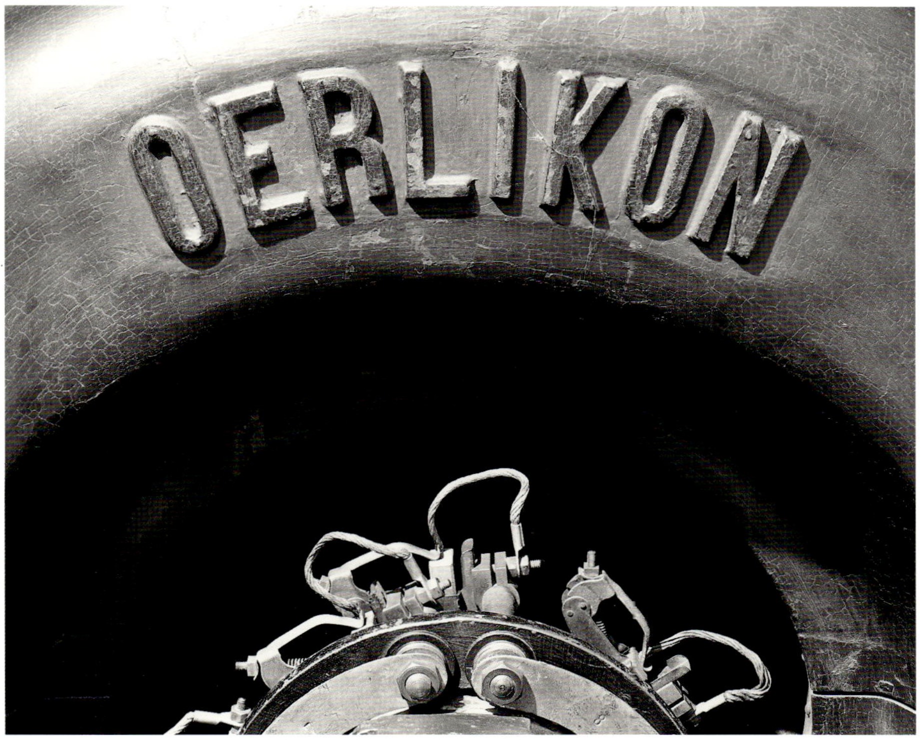
OERLIKON

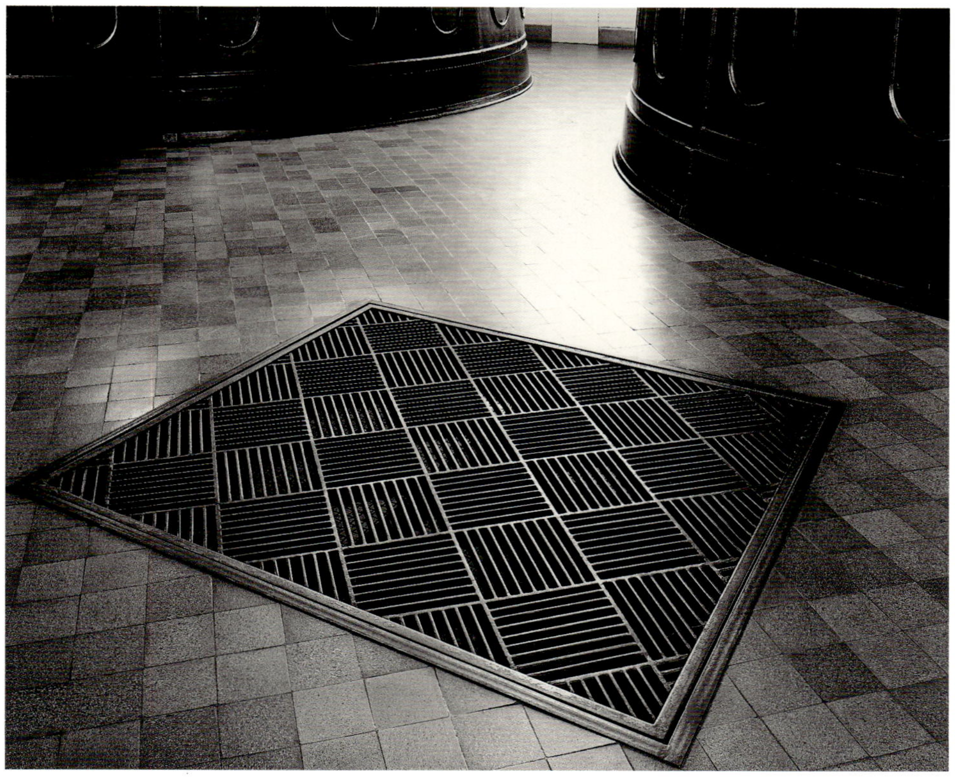

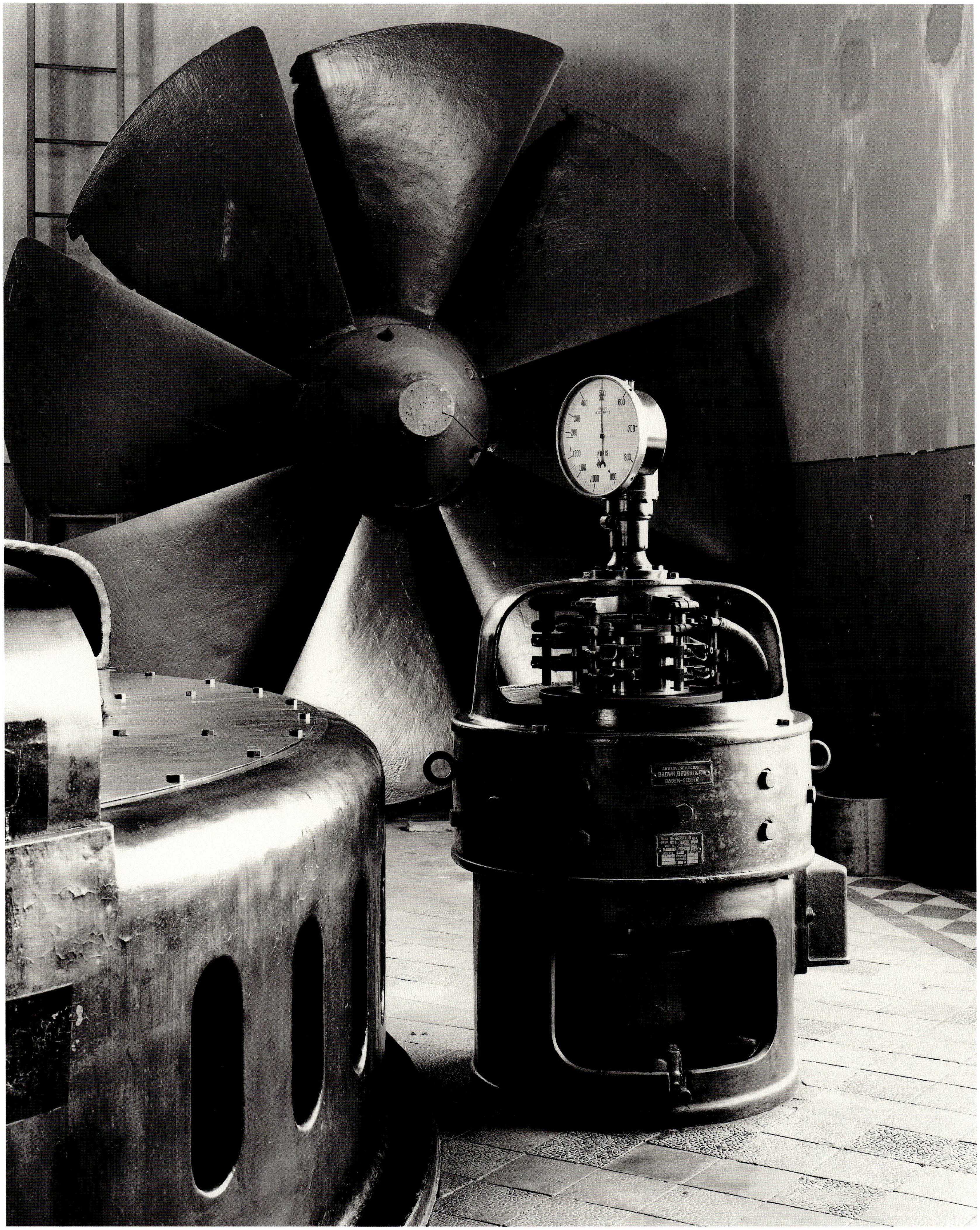
AKTIENGESELLSCHAFT
BROWN, BOVERI & Cie
BADEN-SCHWEIZ
GENERATOR

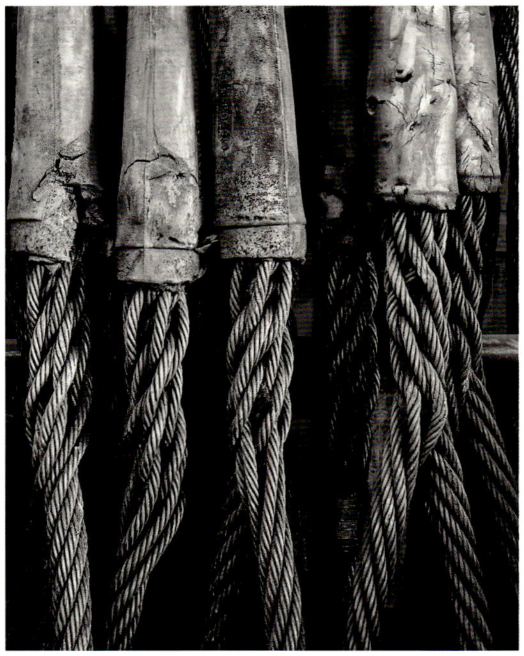

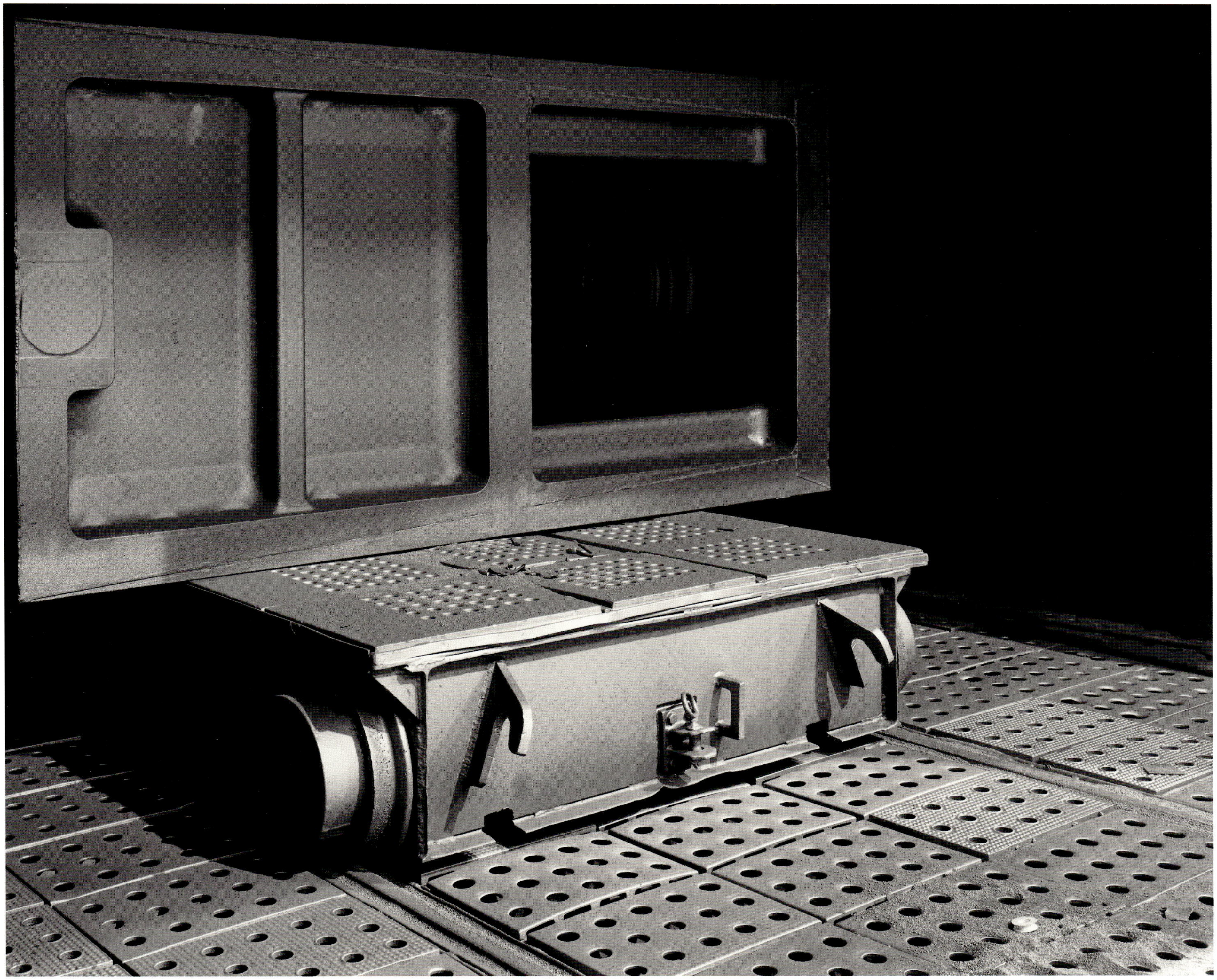

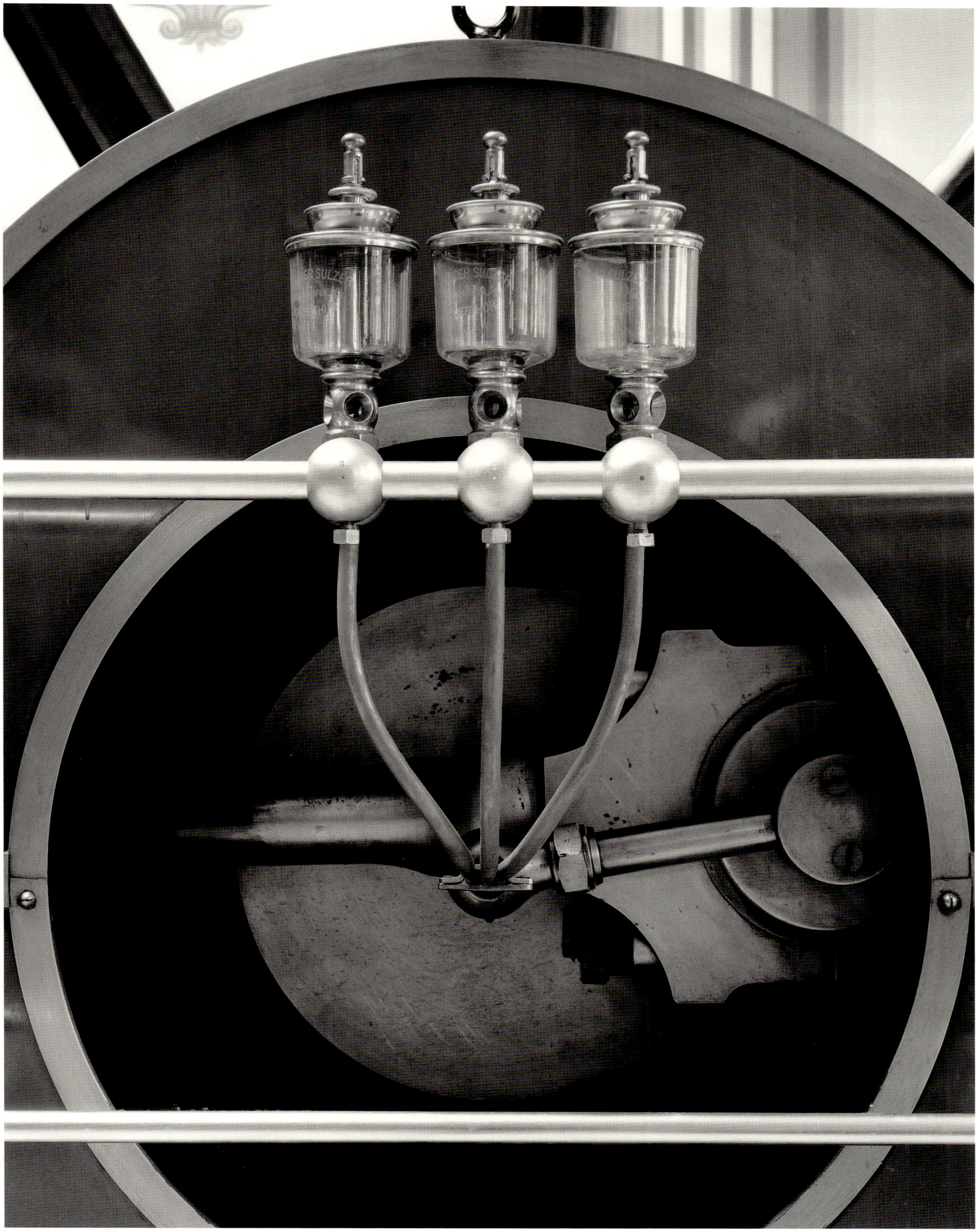

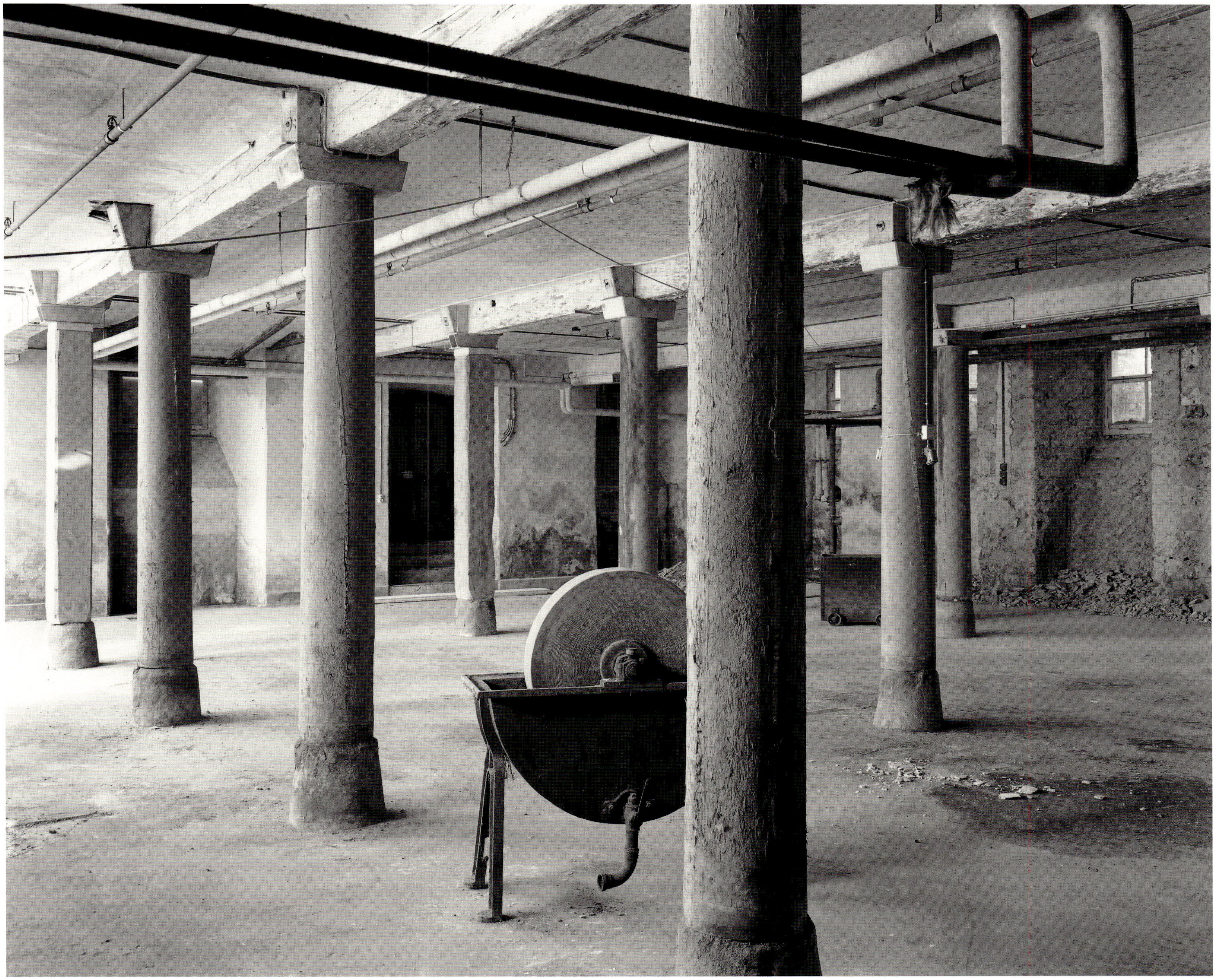

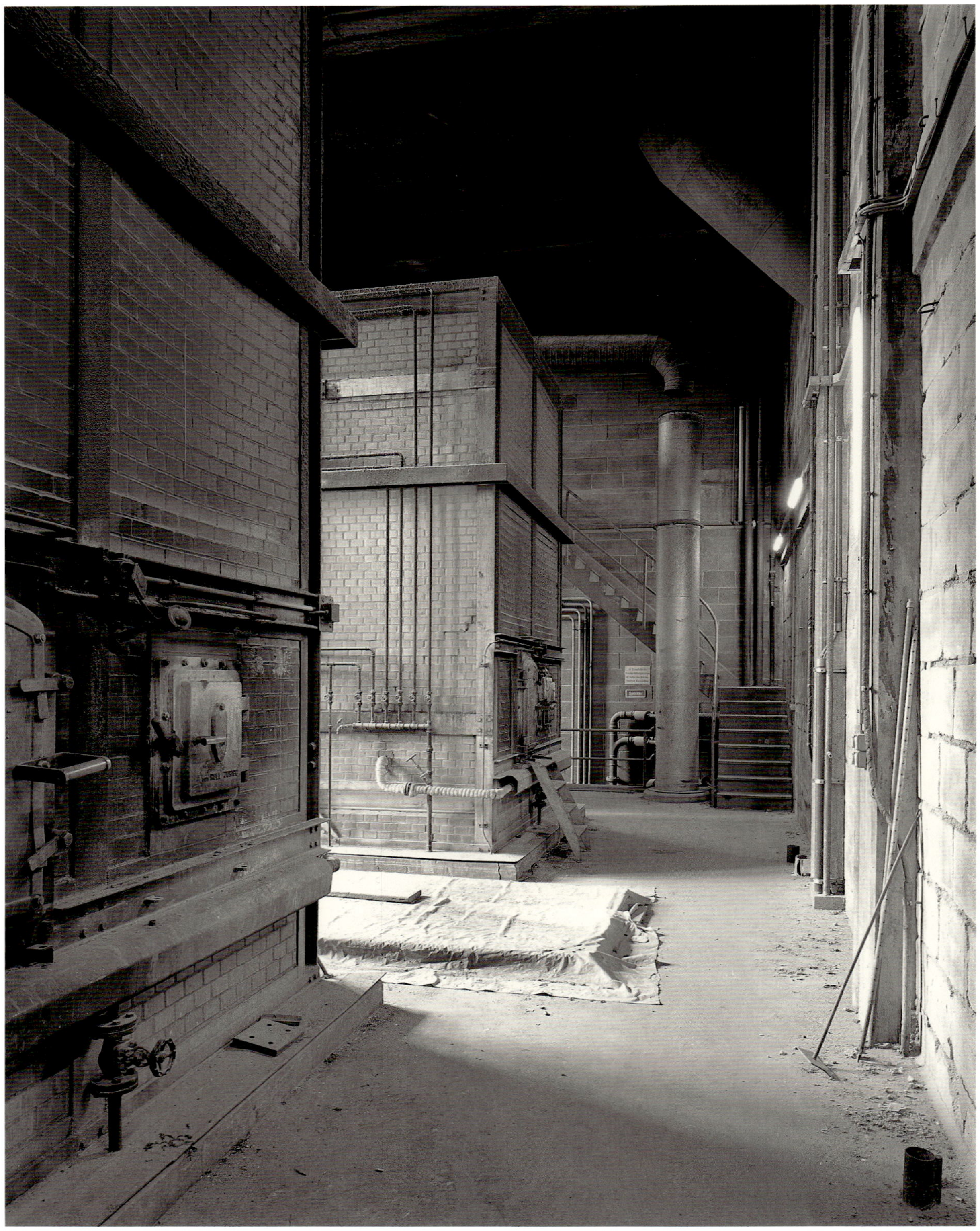

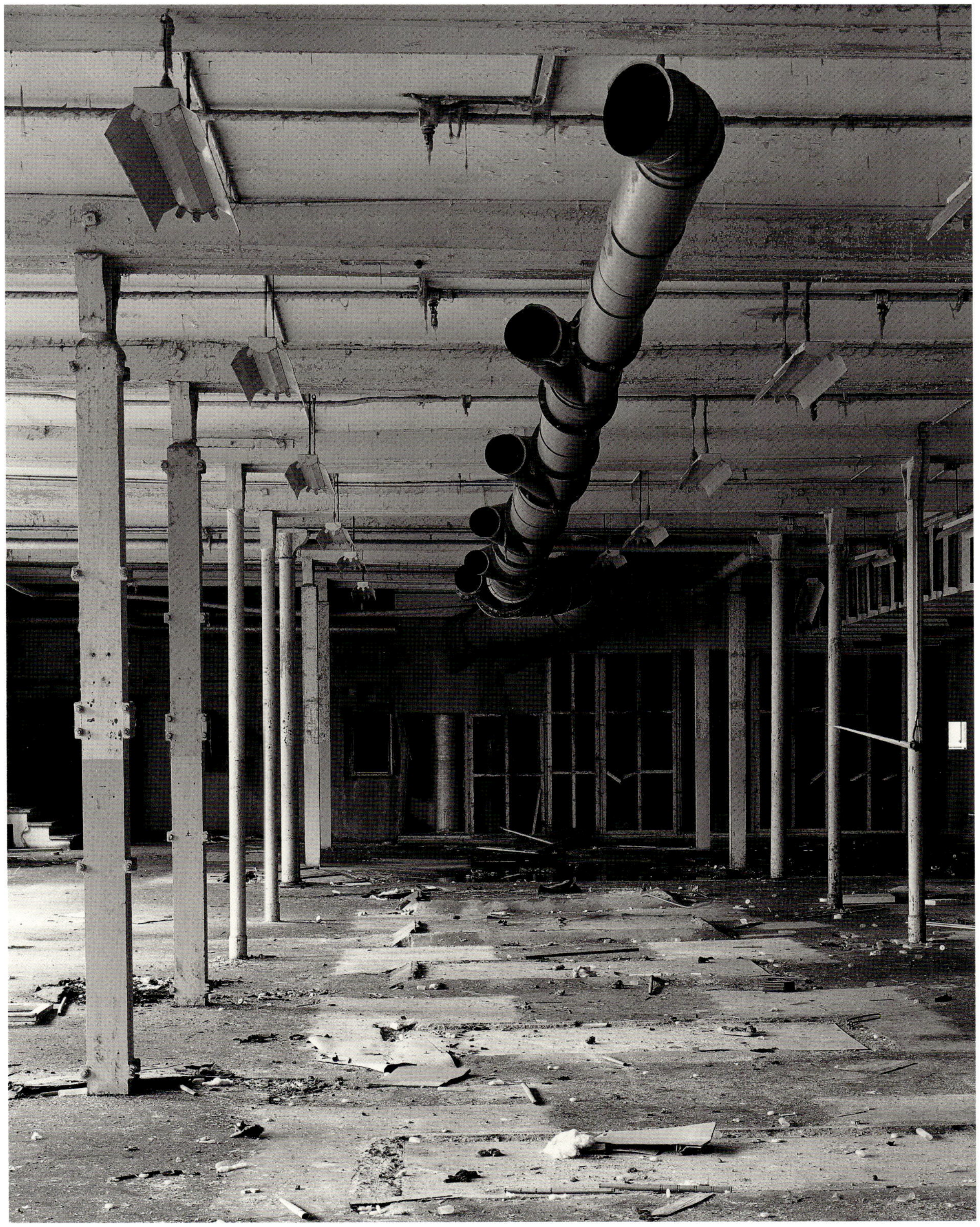

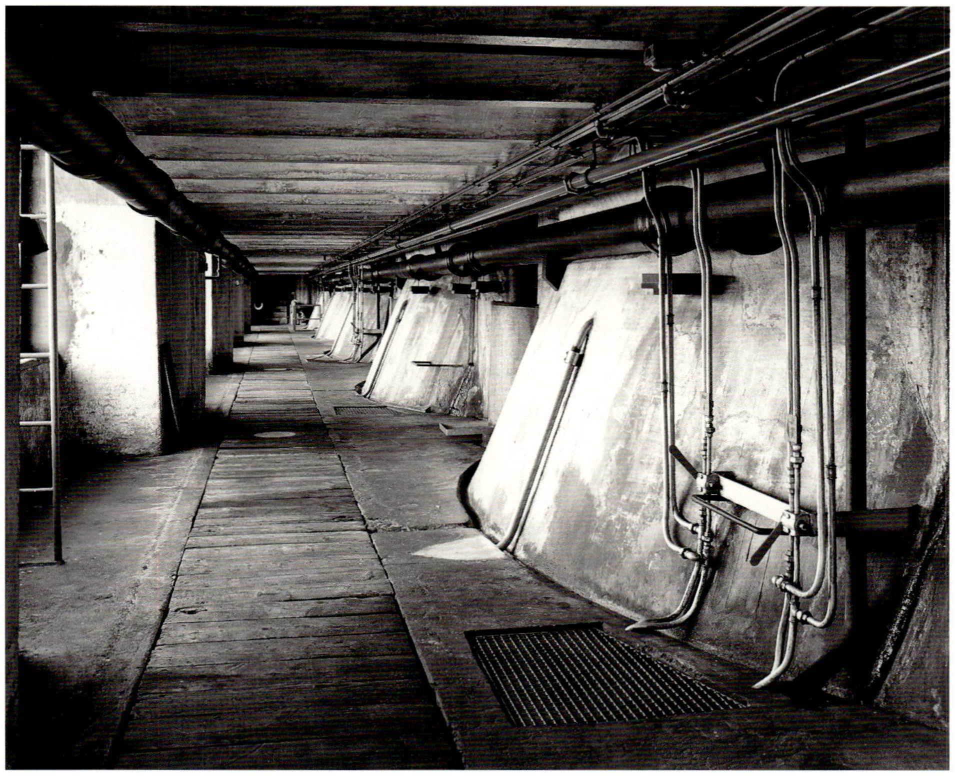

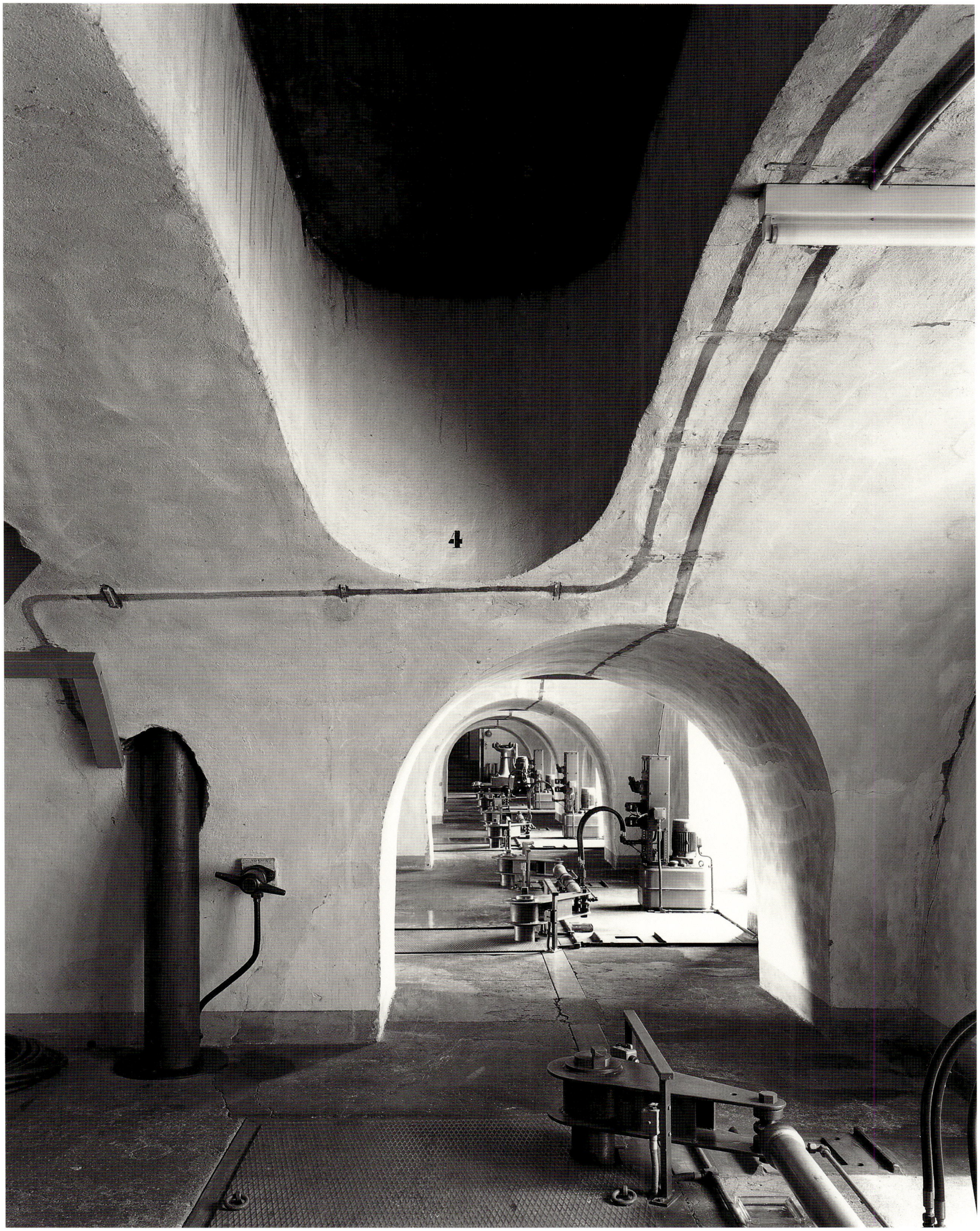
4

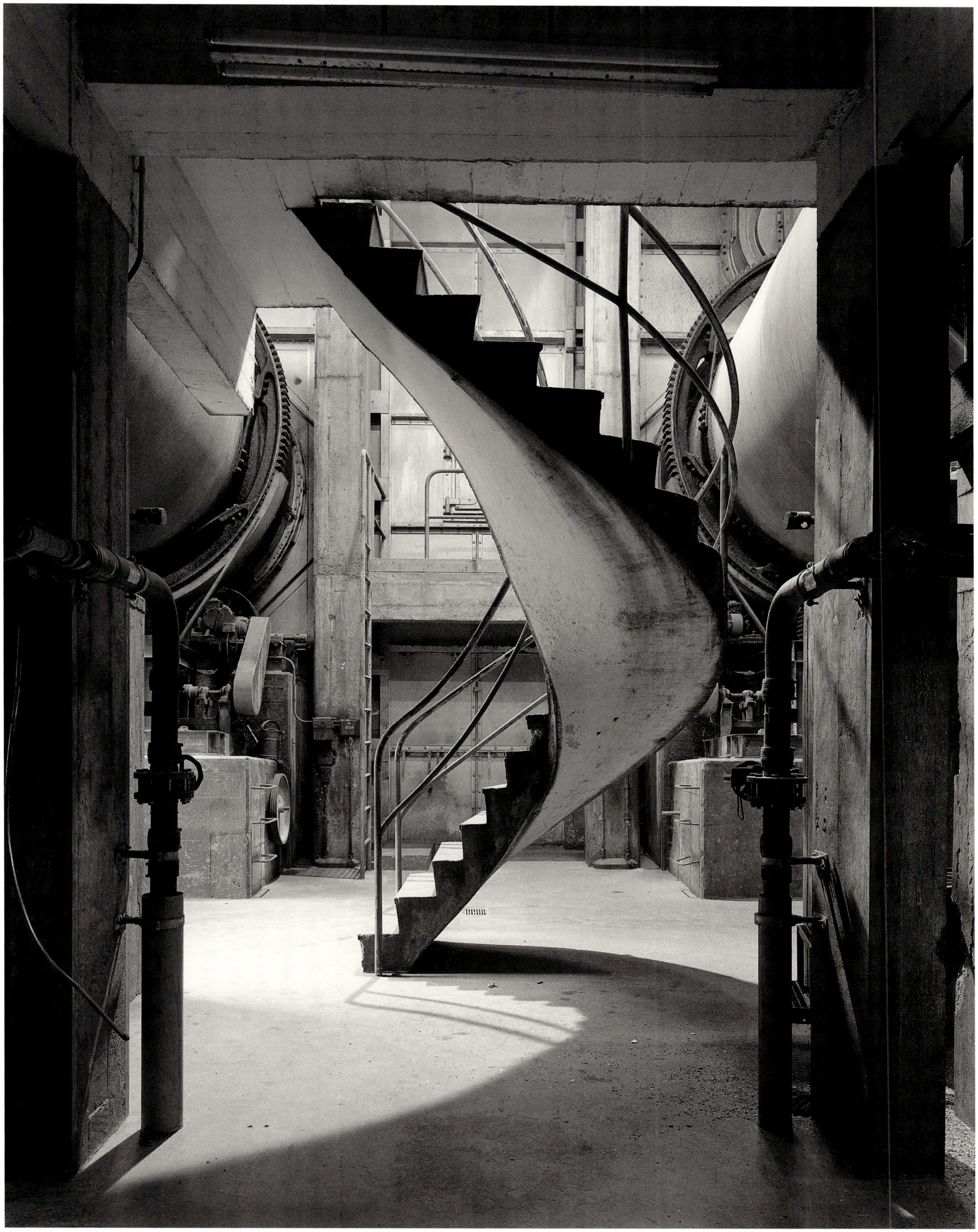

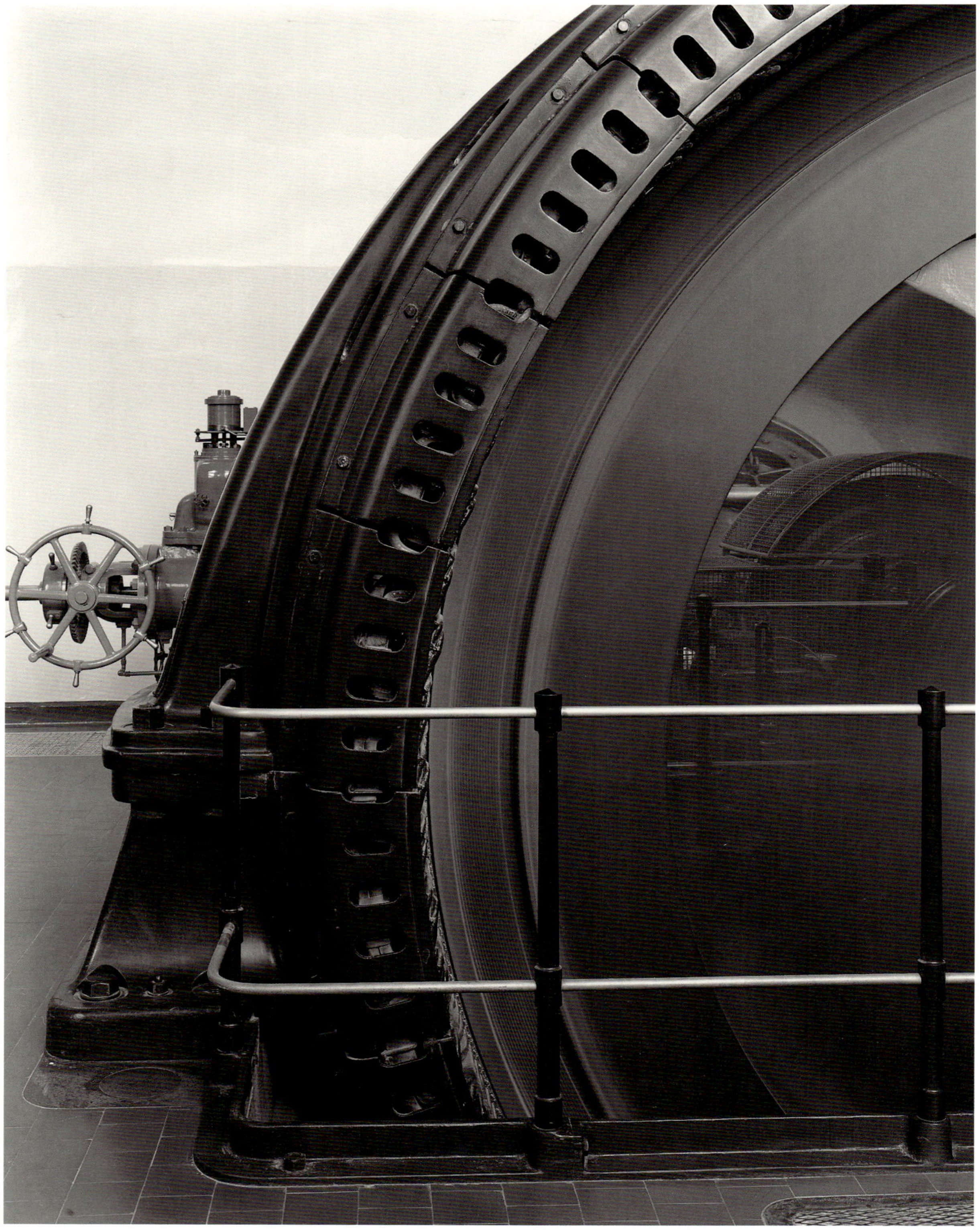

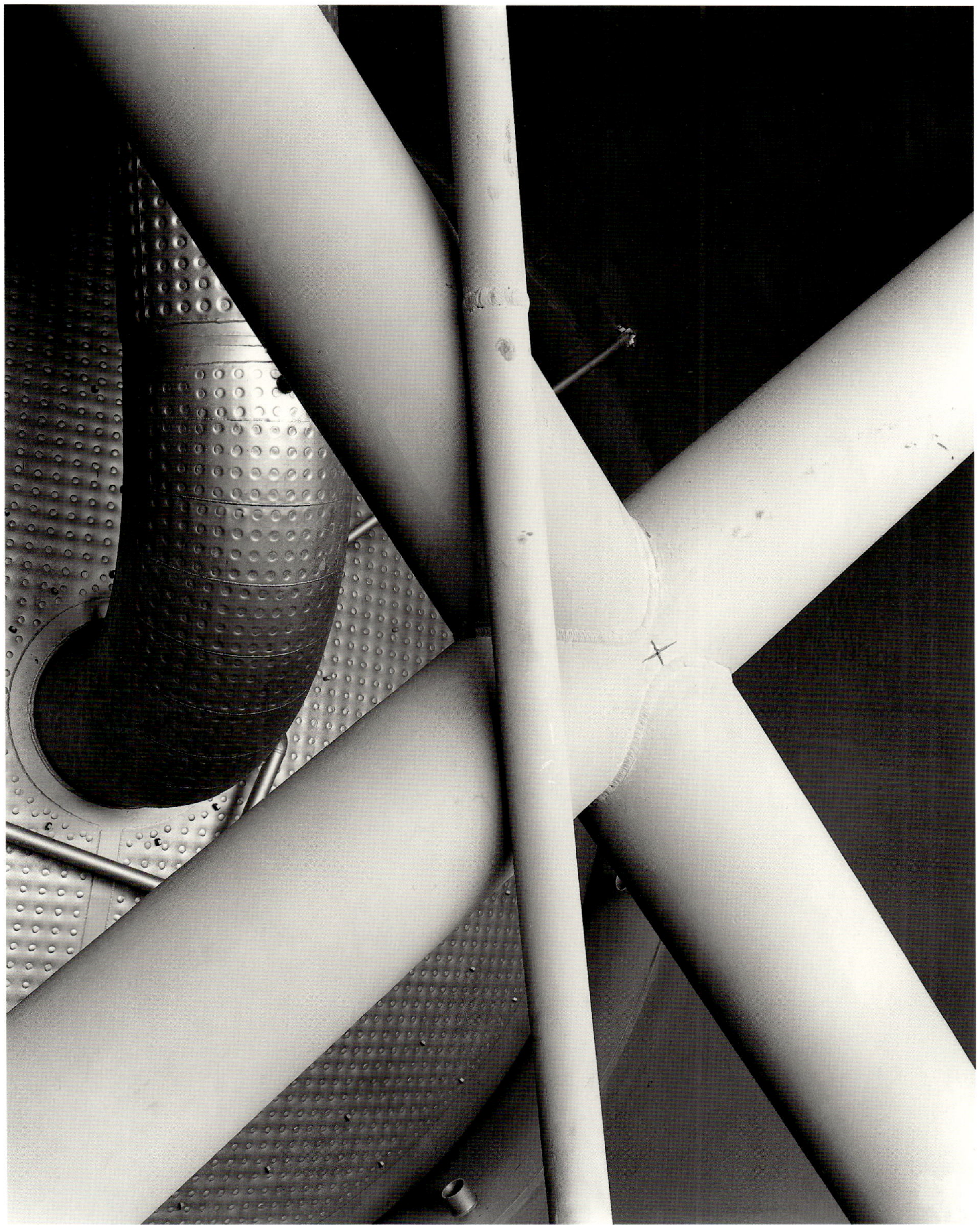

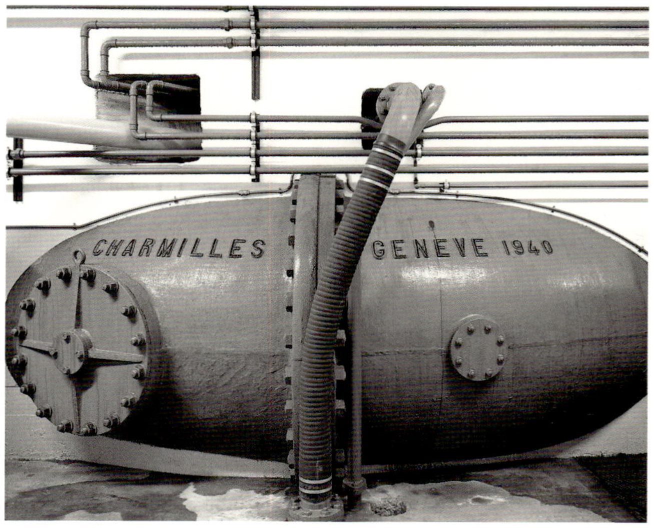
CHARMILLES
GENEVE 1940

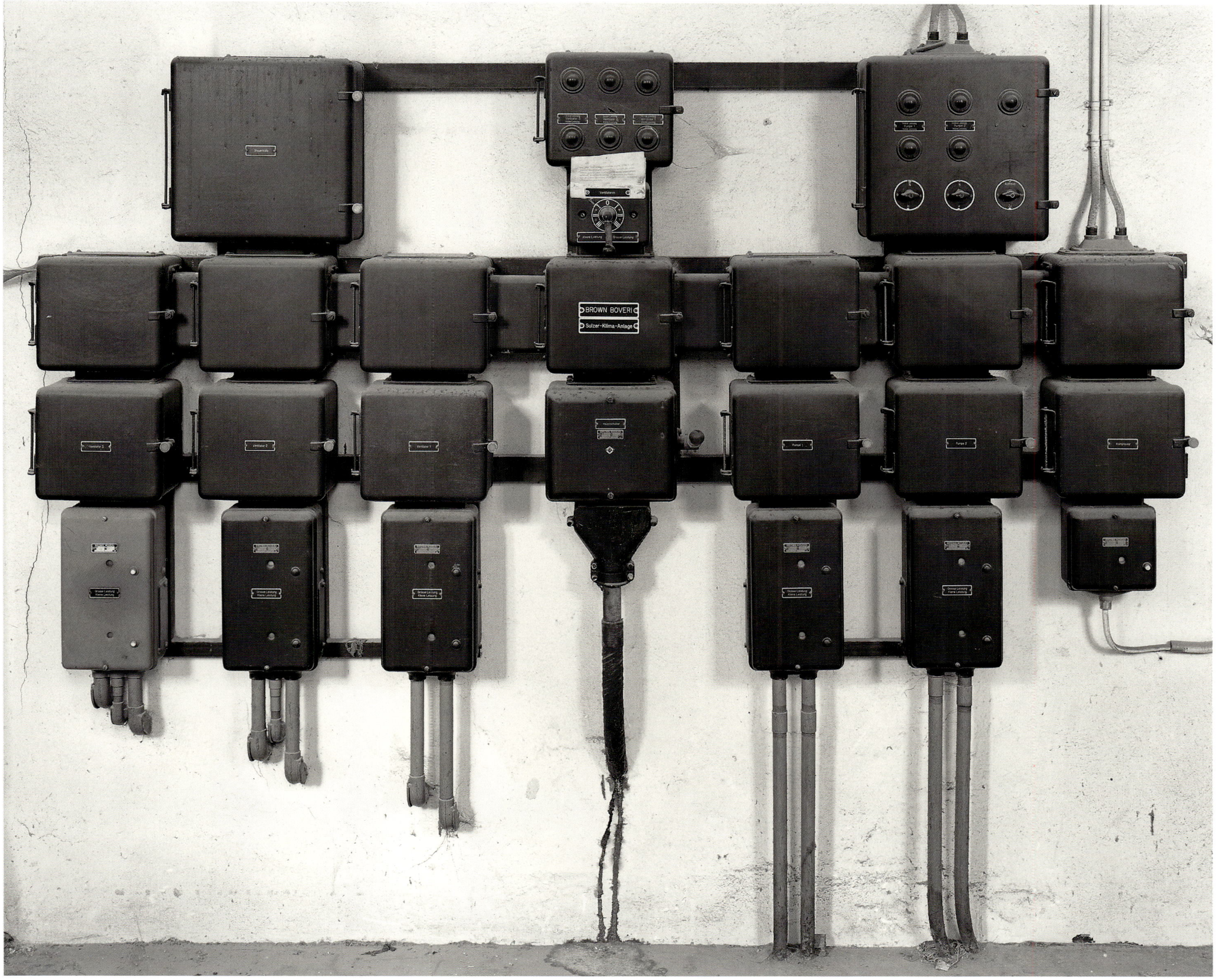
BROWN BOVERI
Sulzer-Klima-Anlage

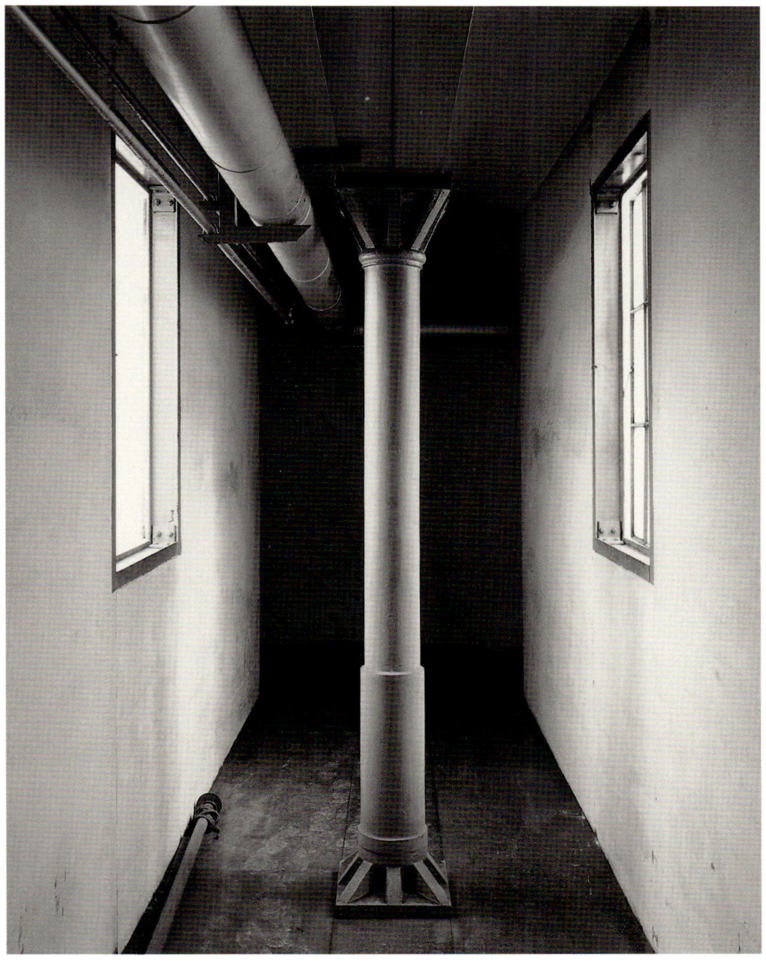

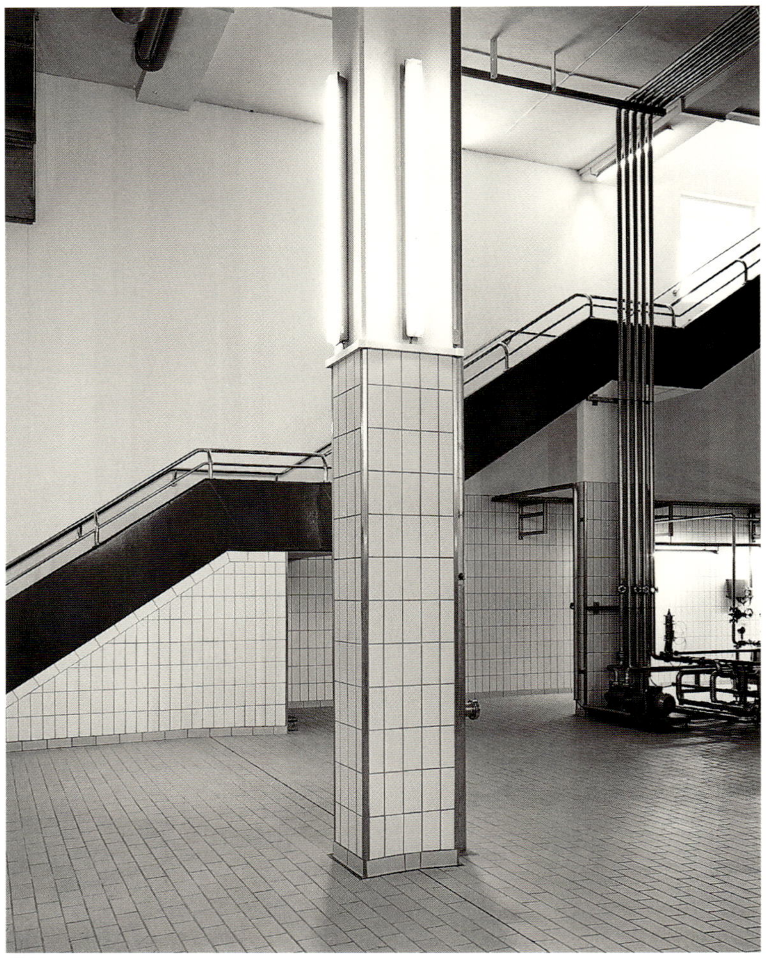

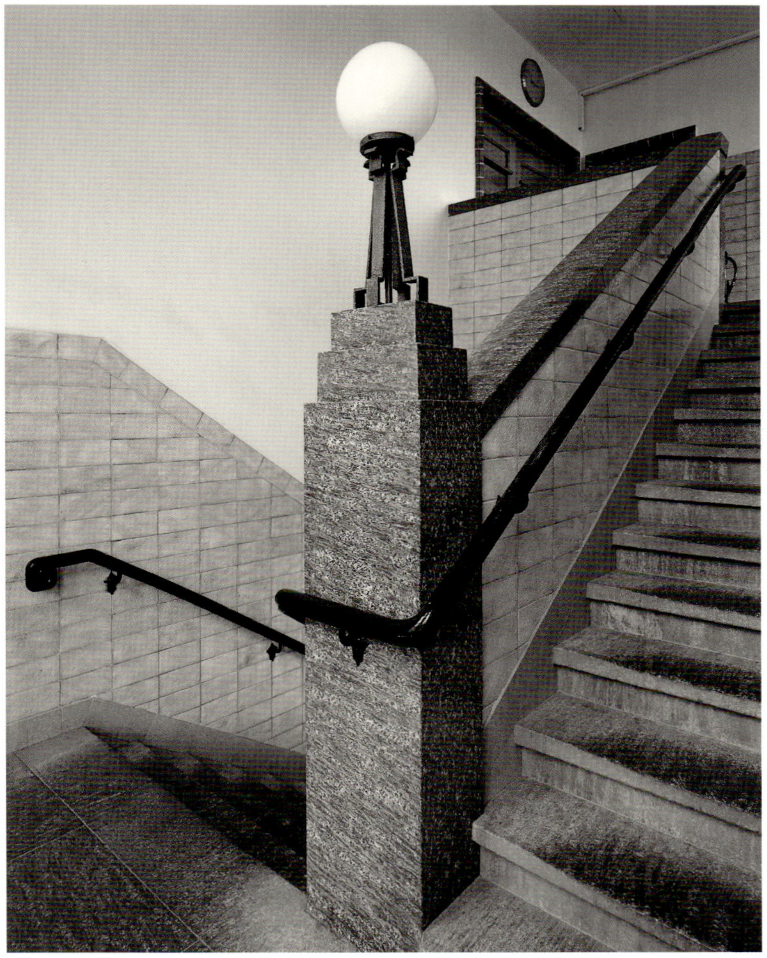

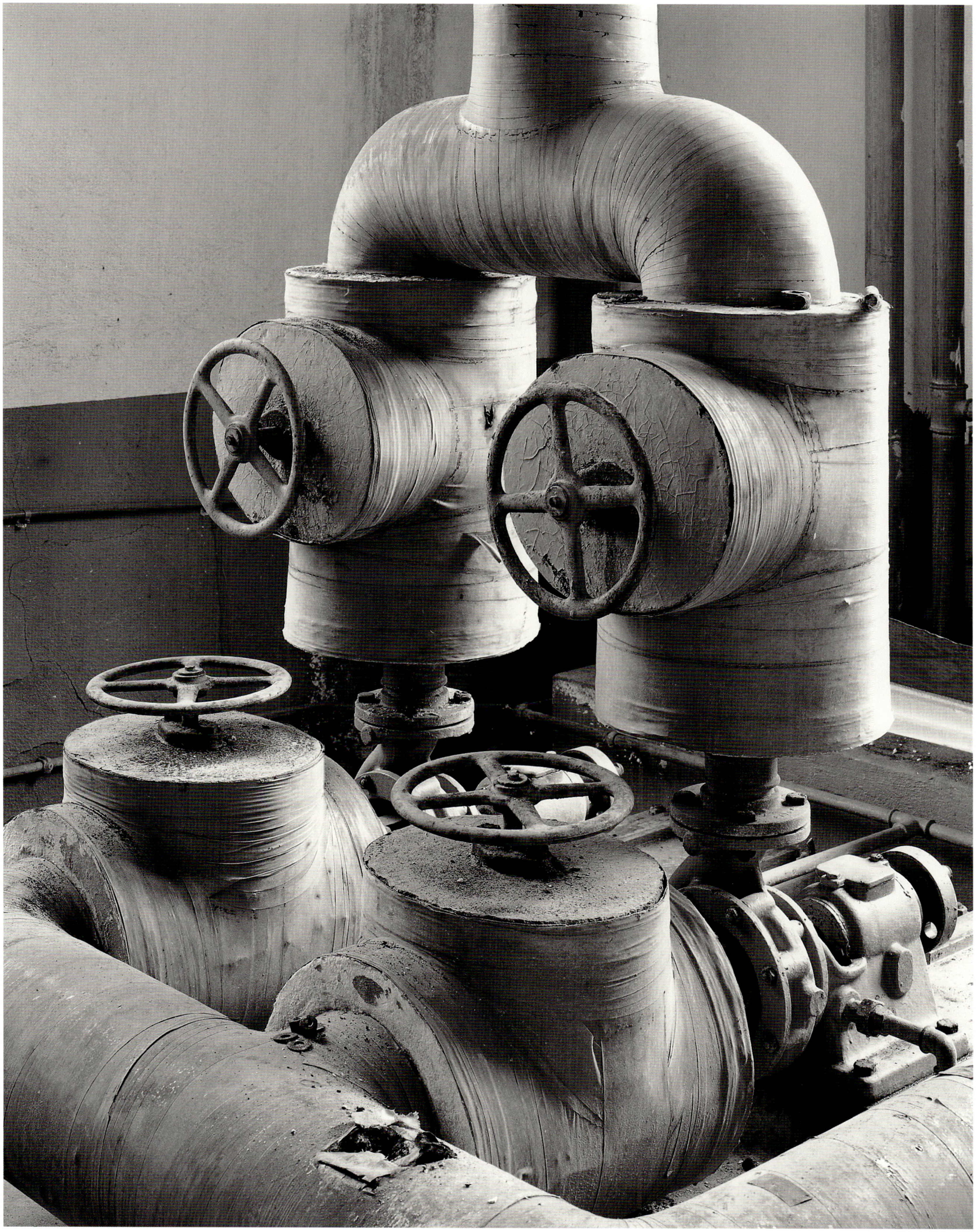

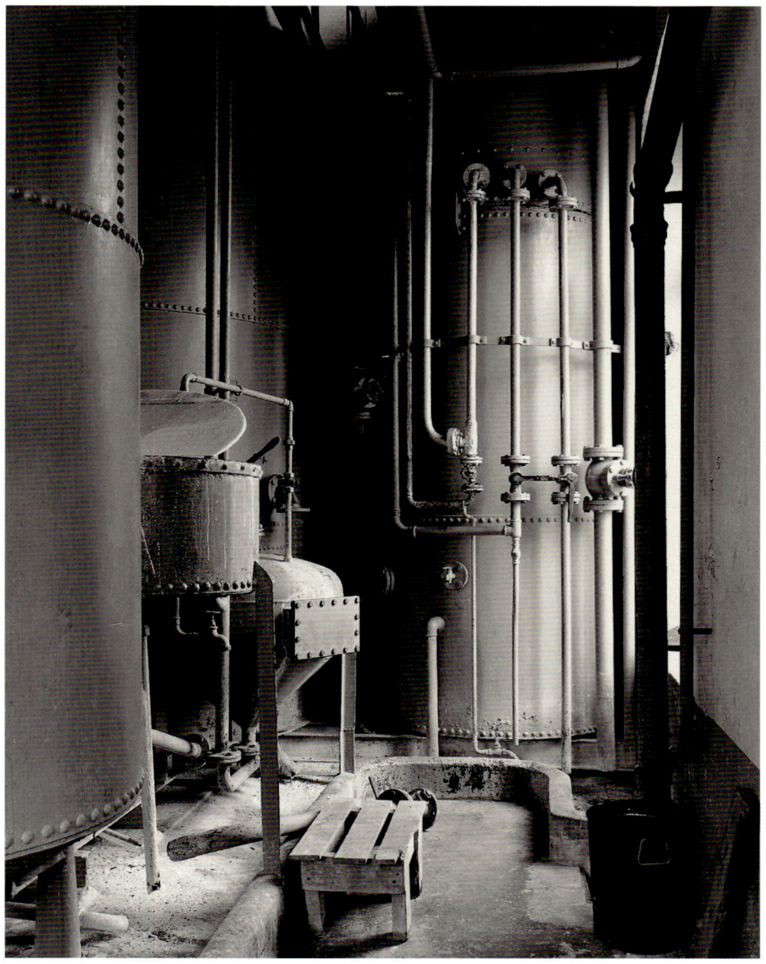

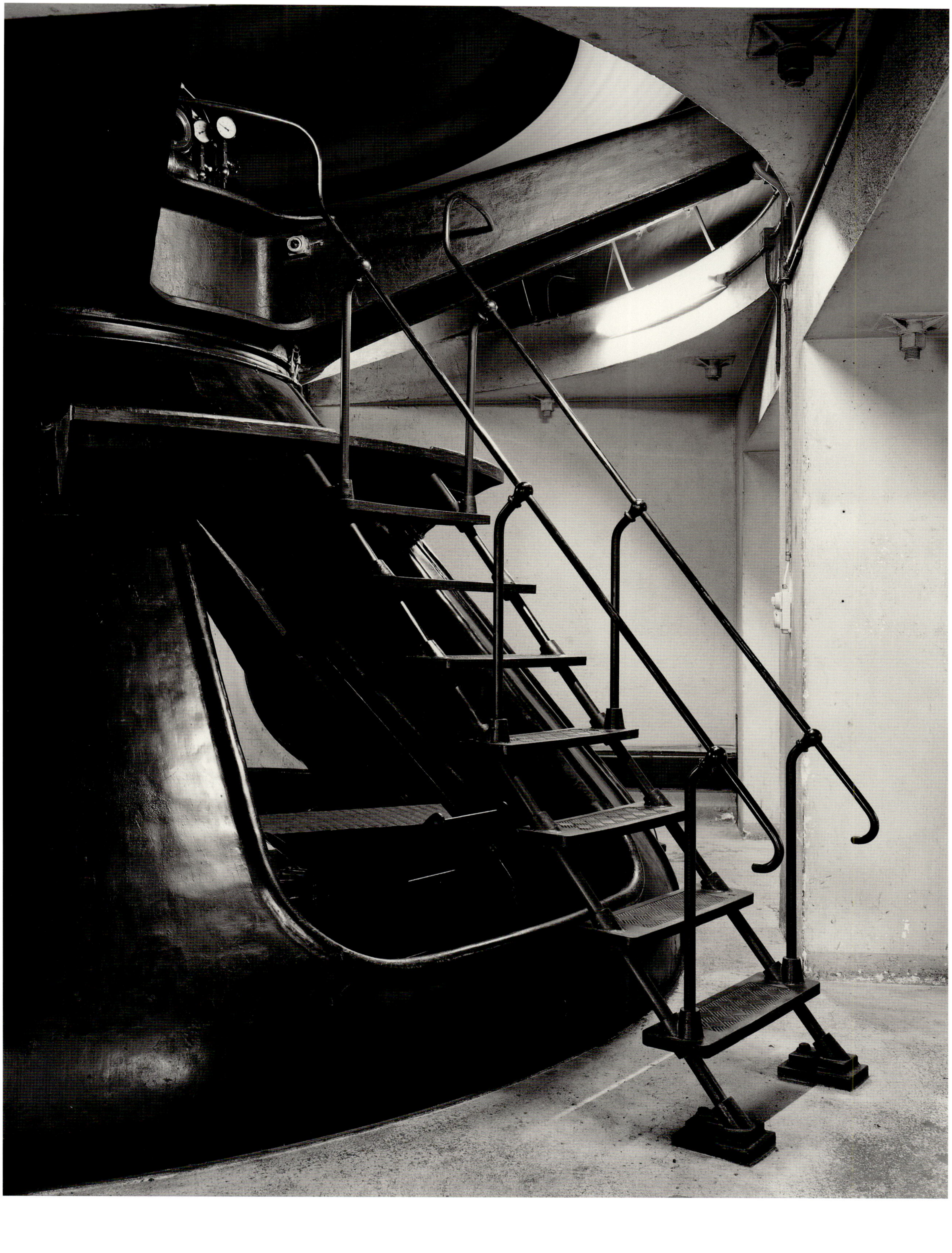

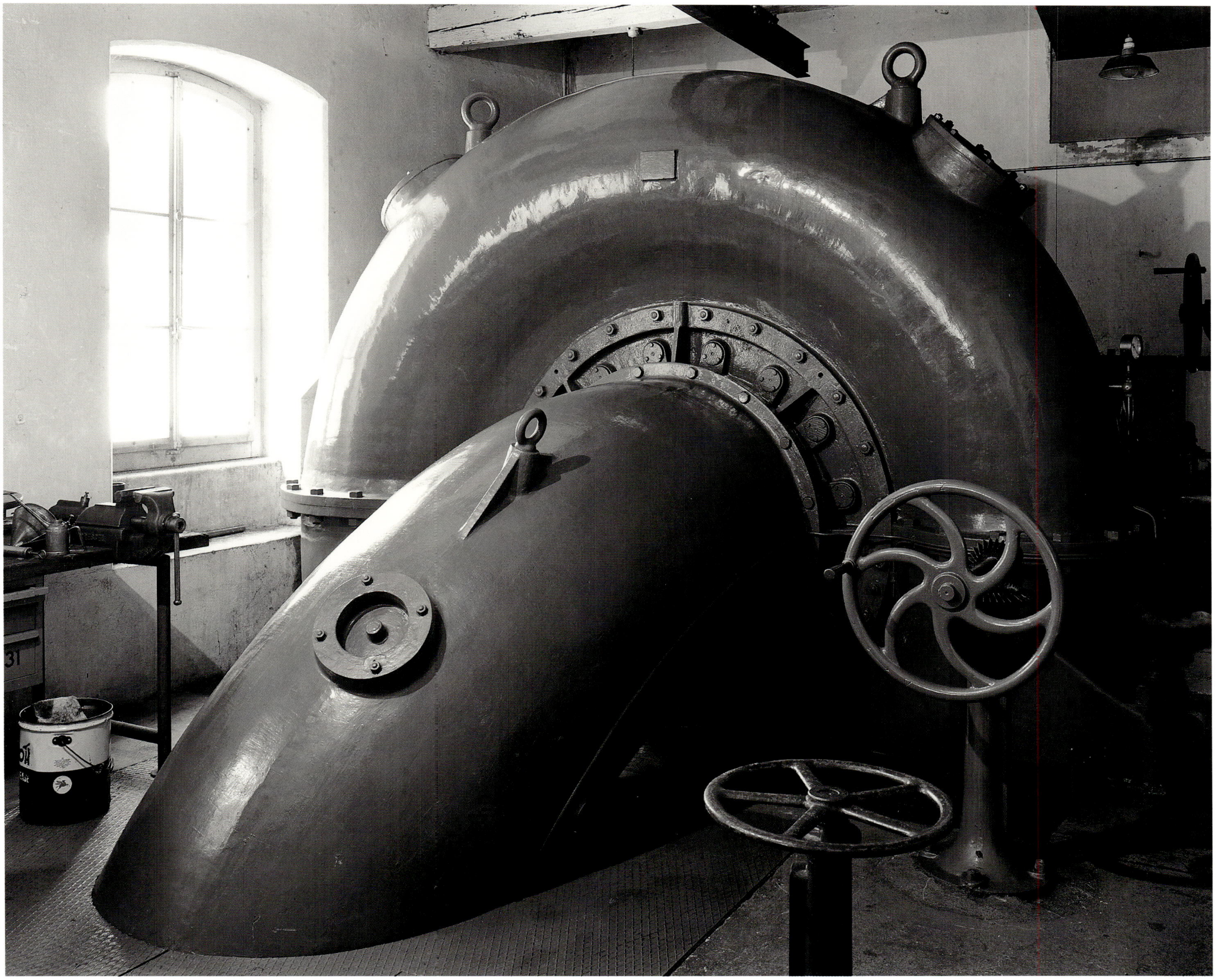

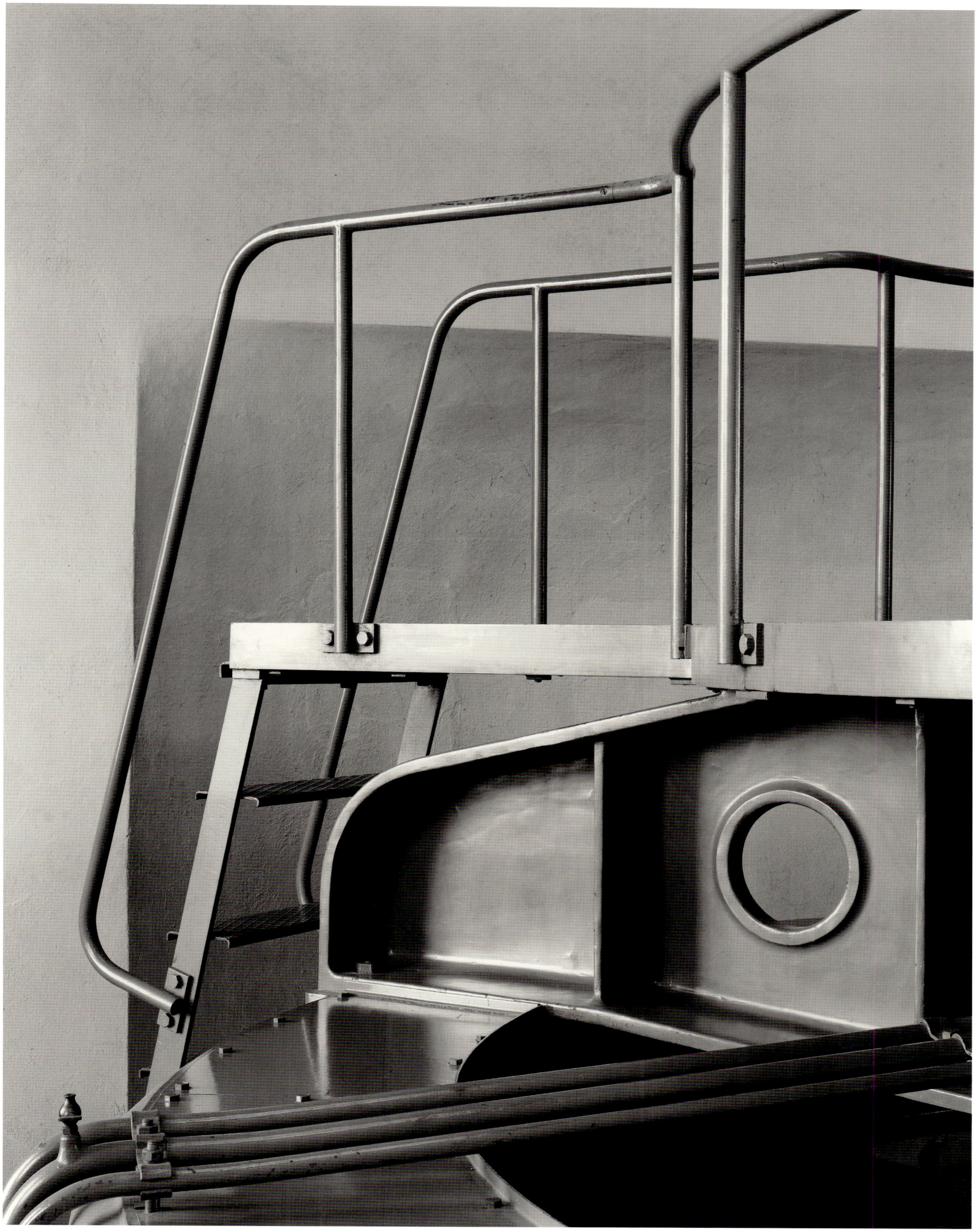

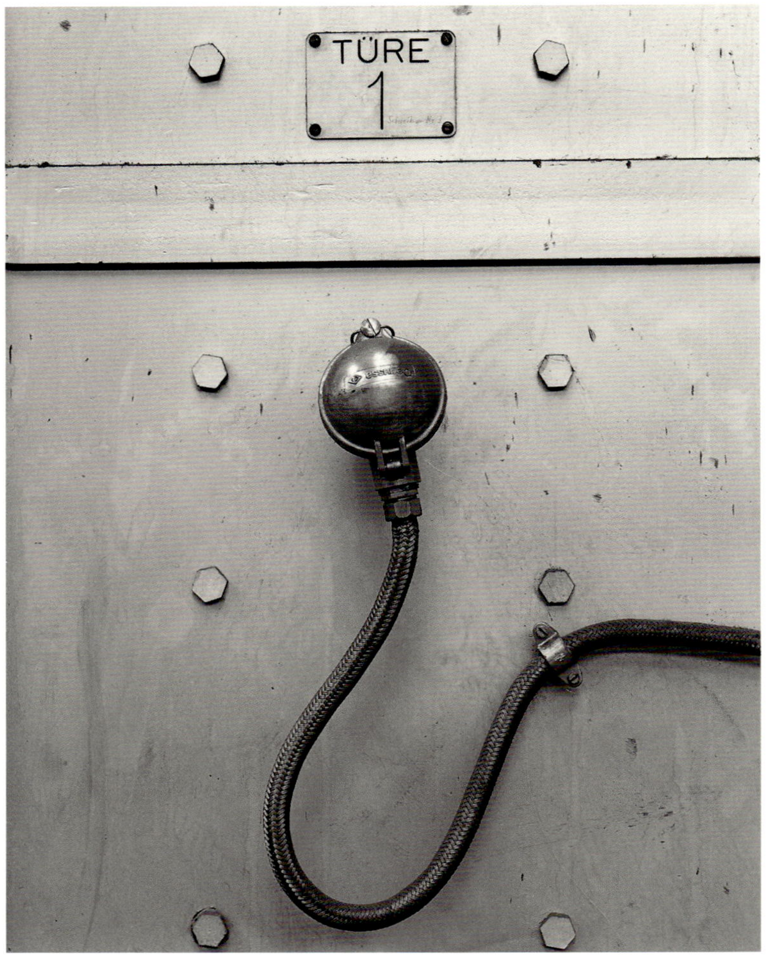
TÜRE
1

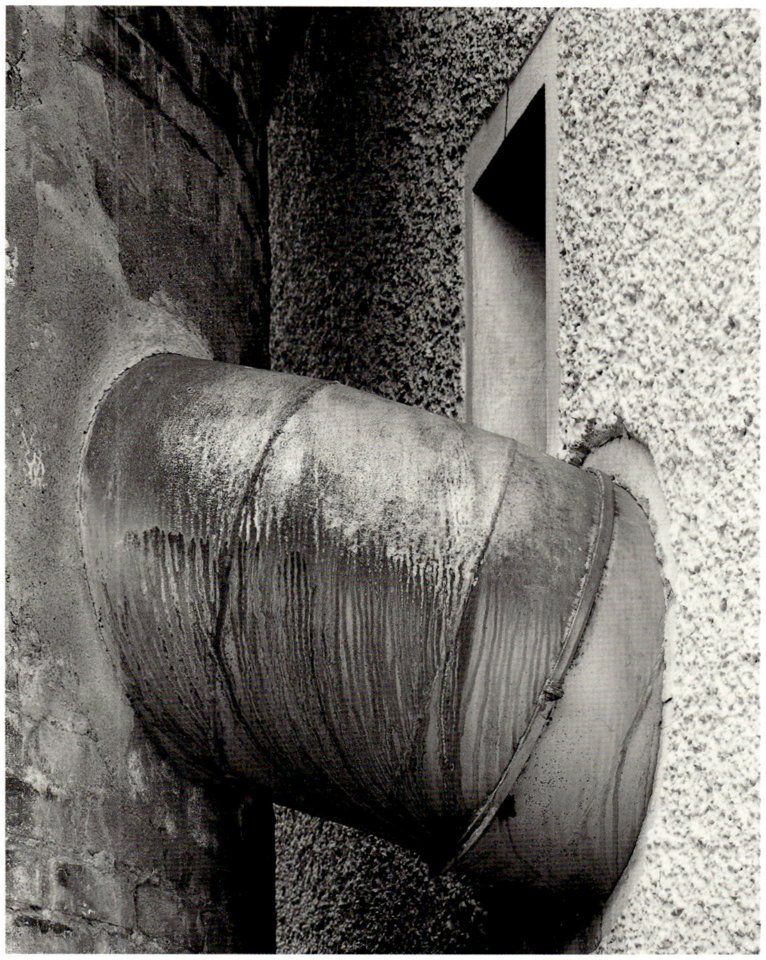

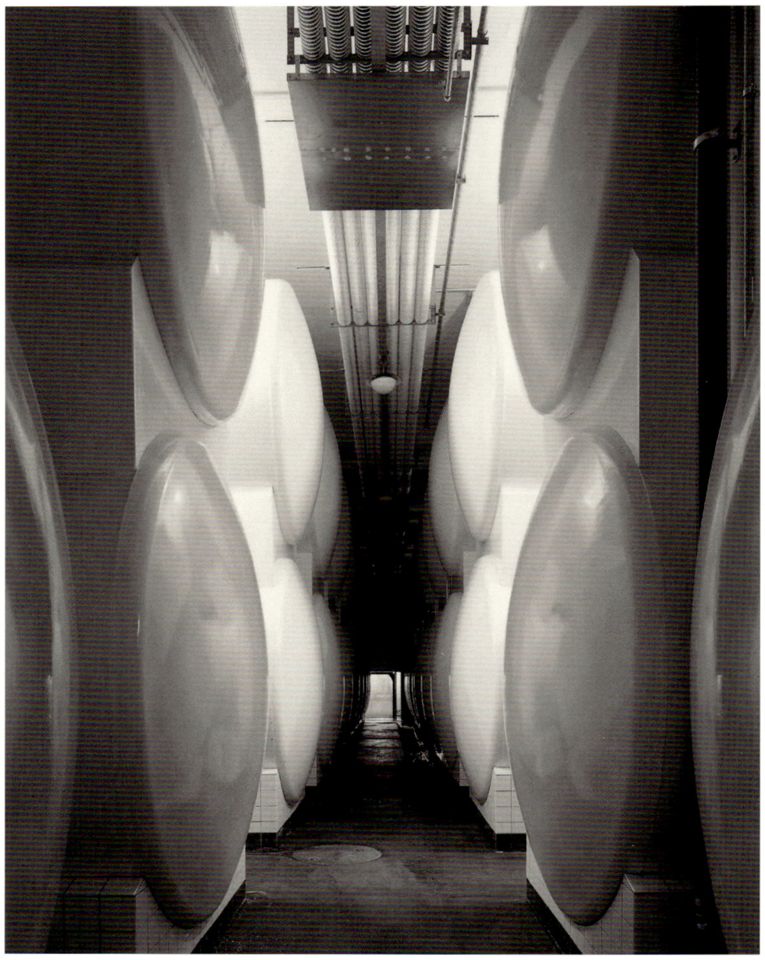

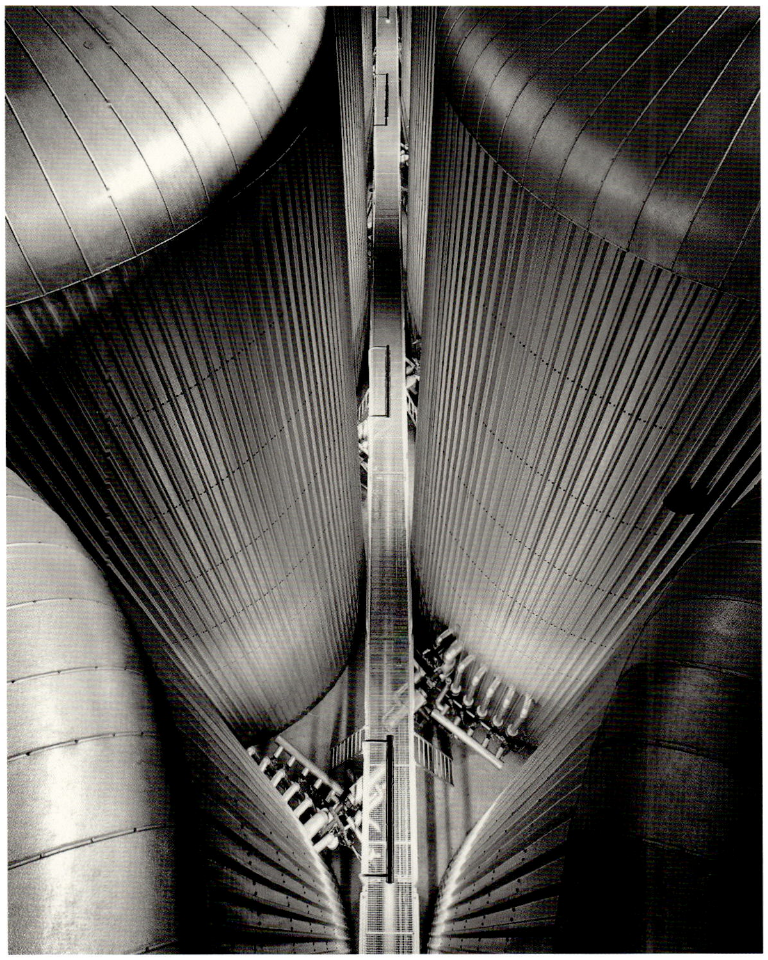

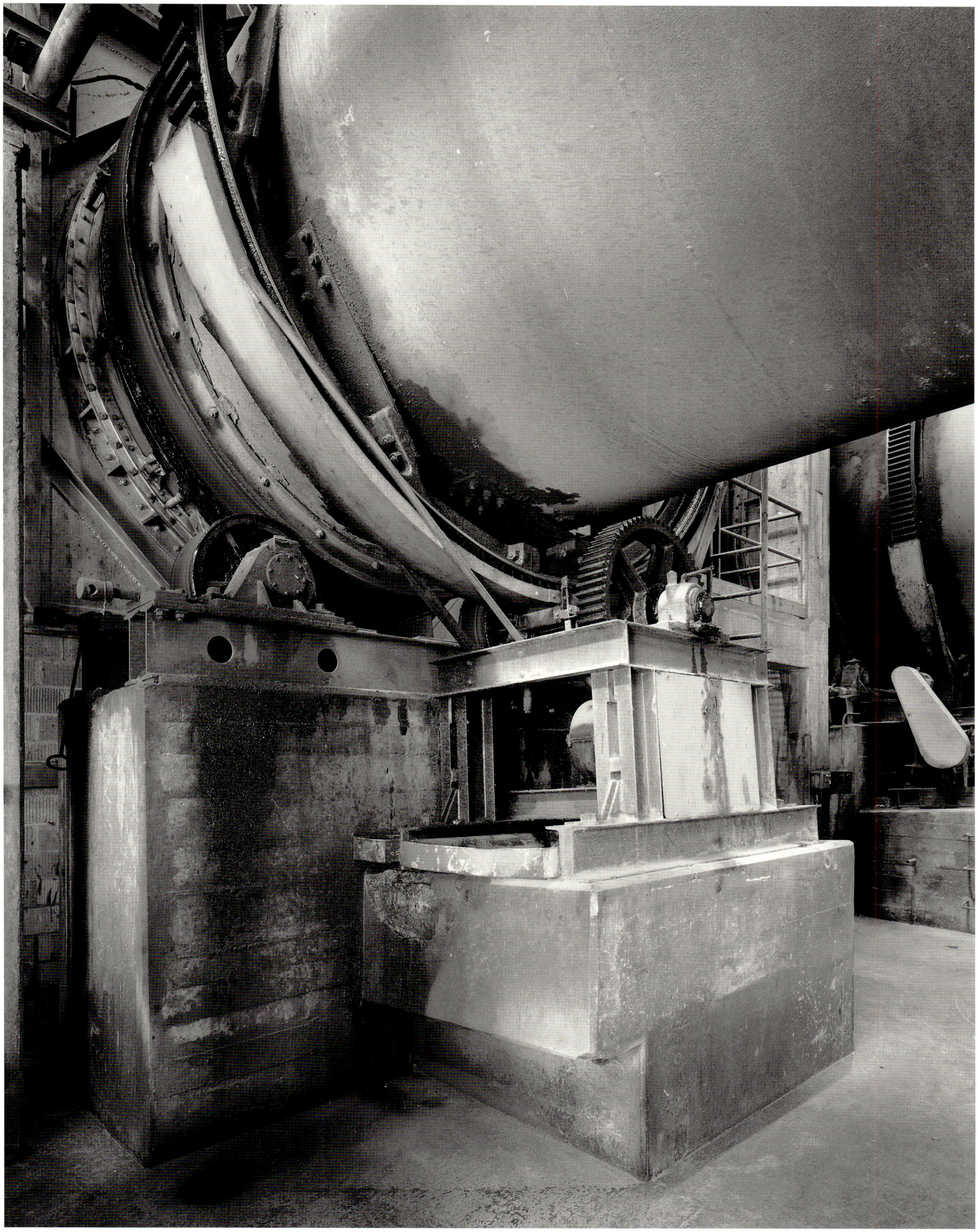

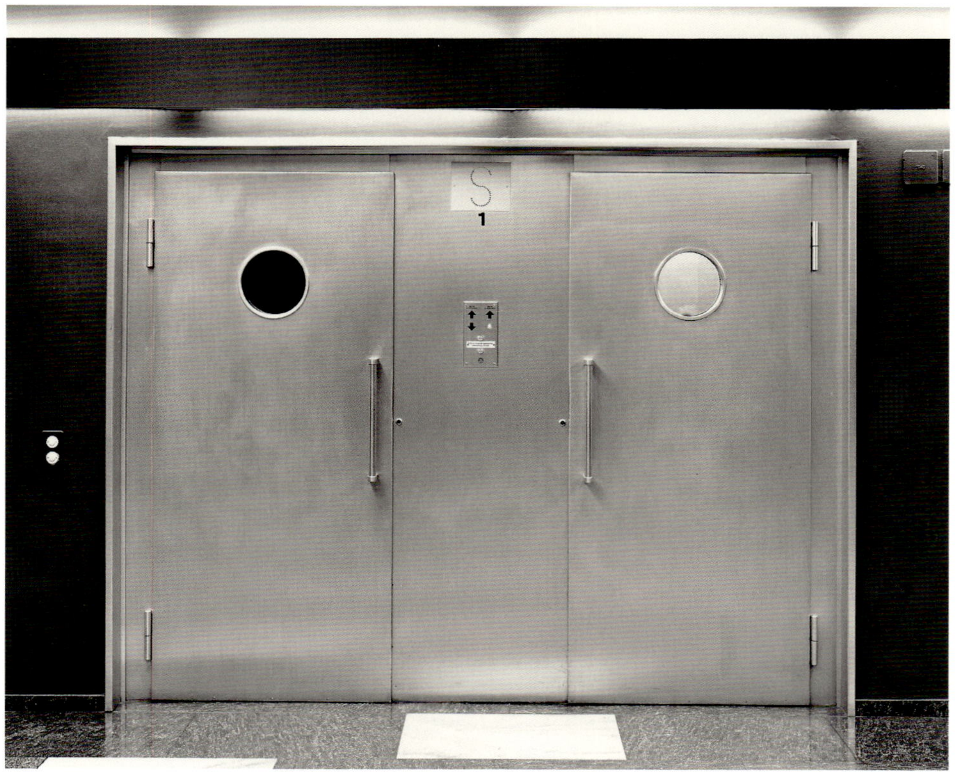
S
1

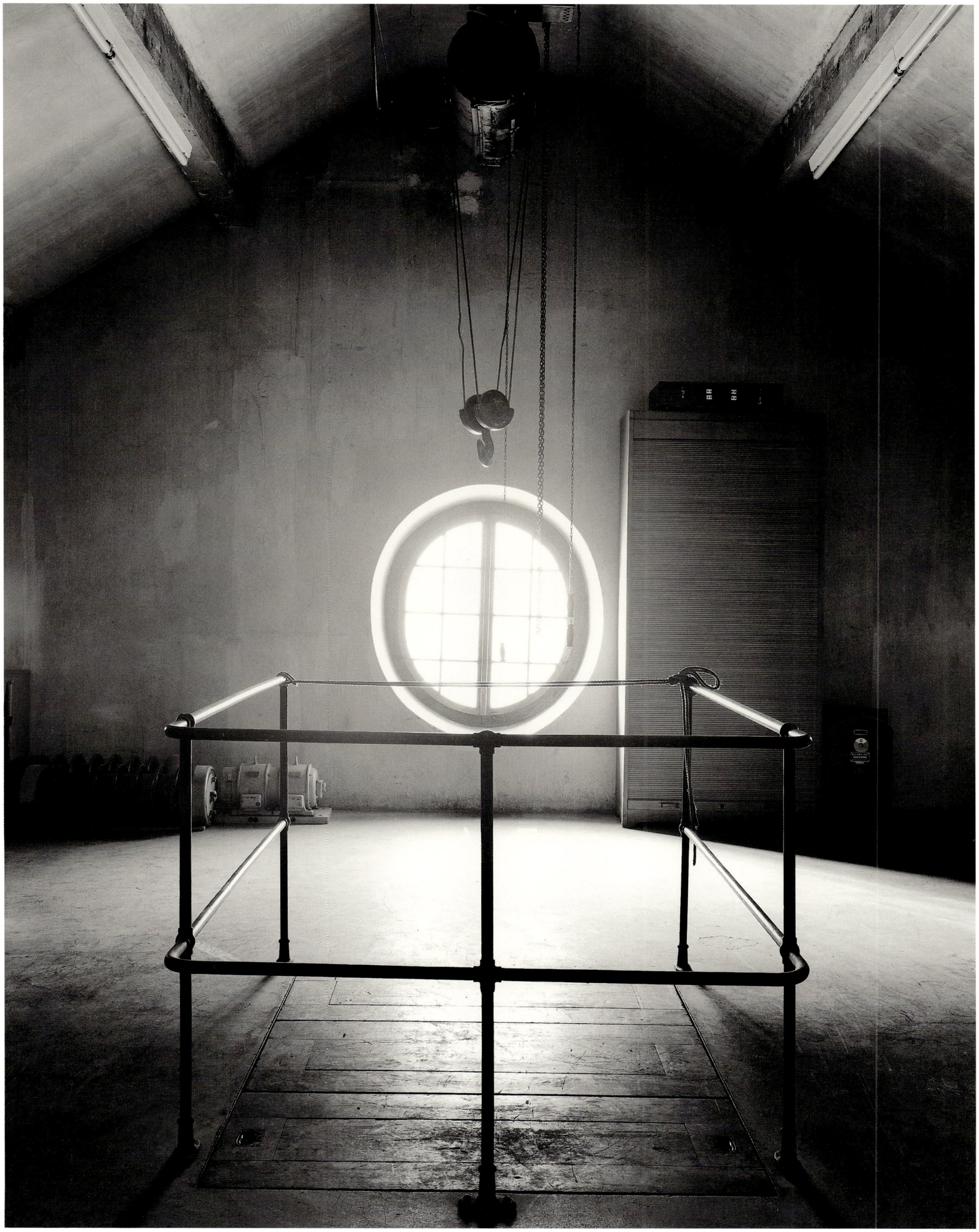

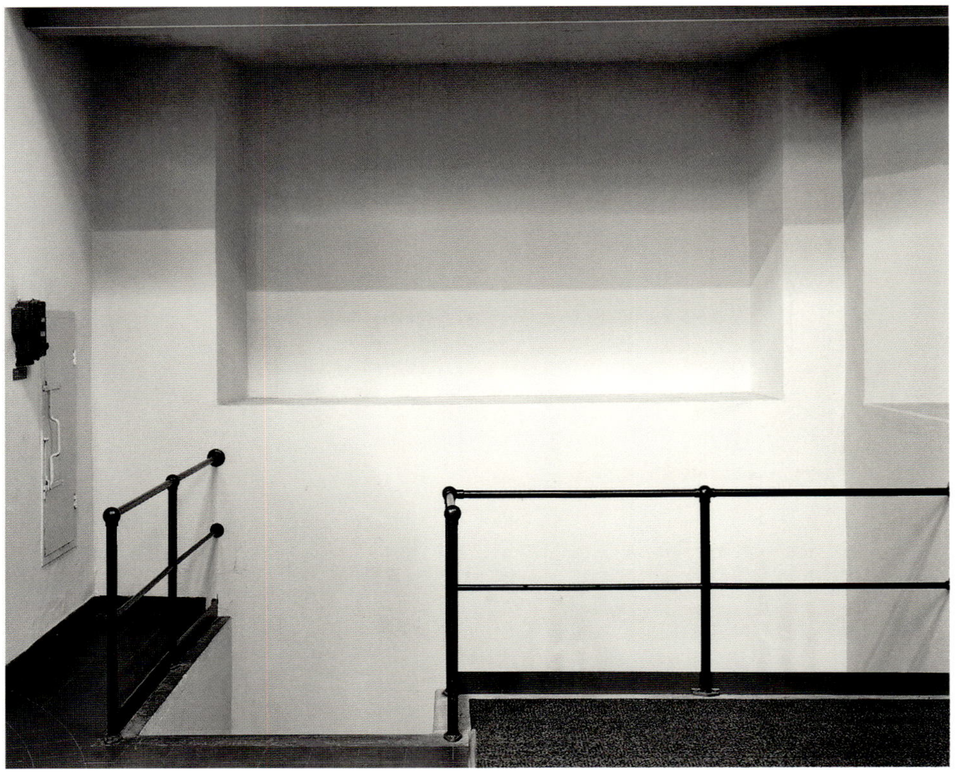

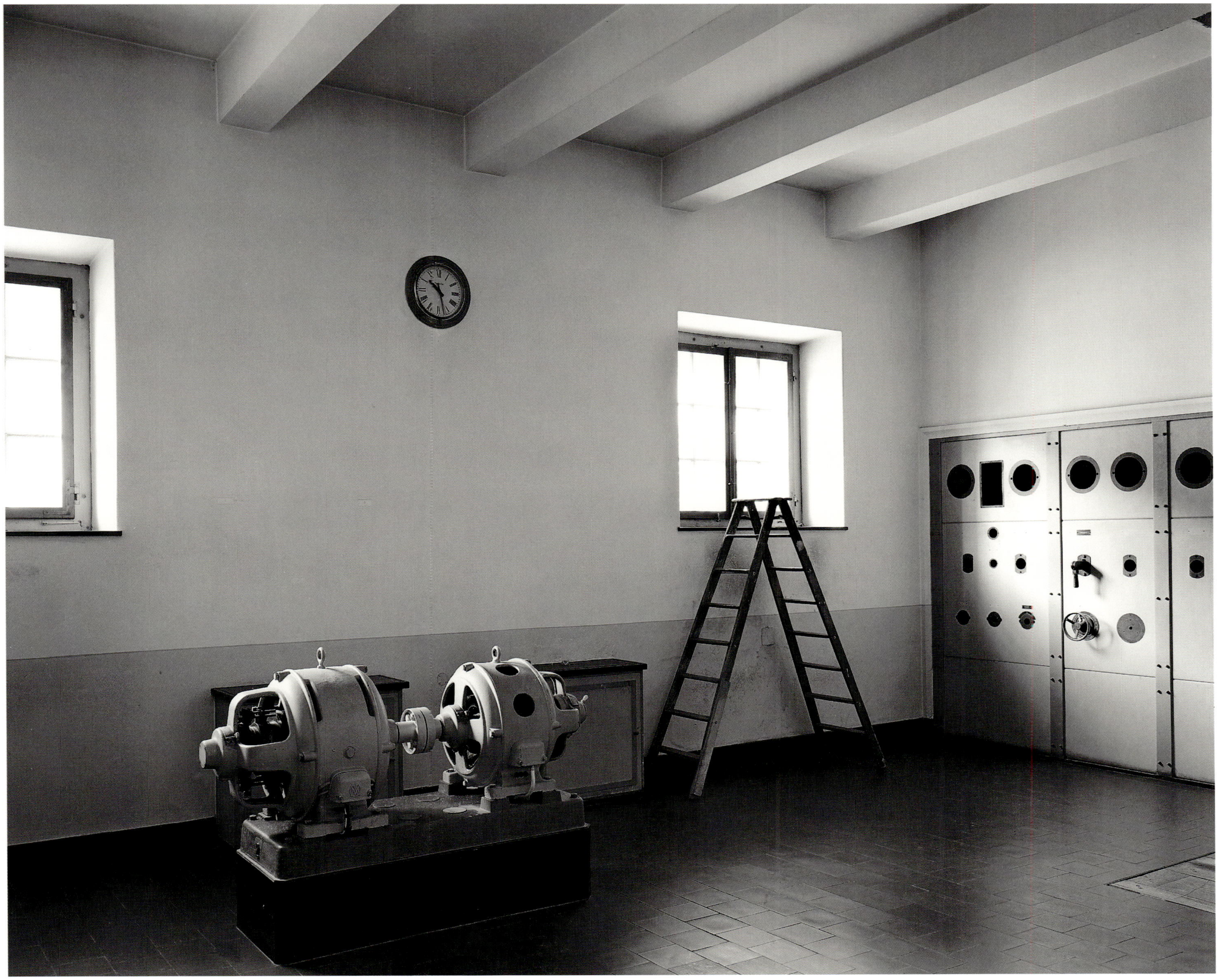

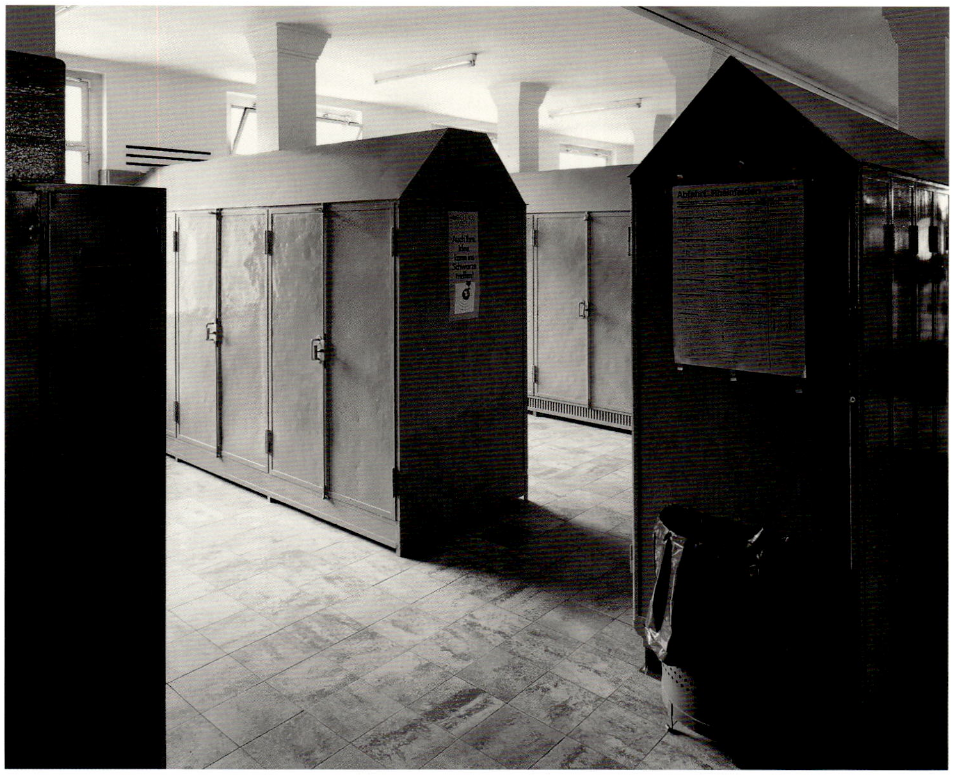

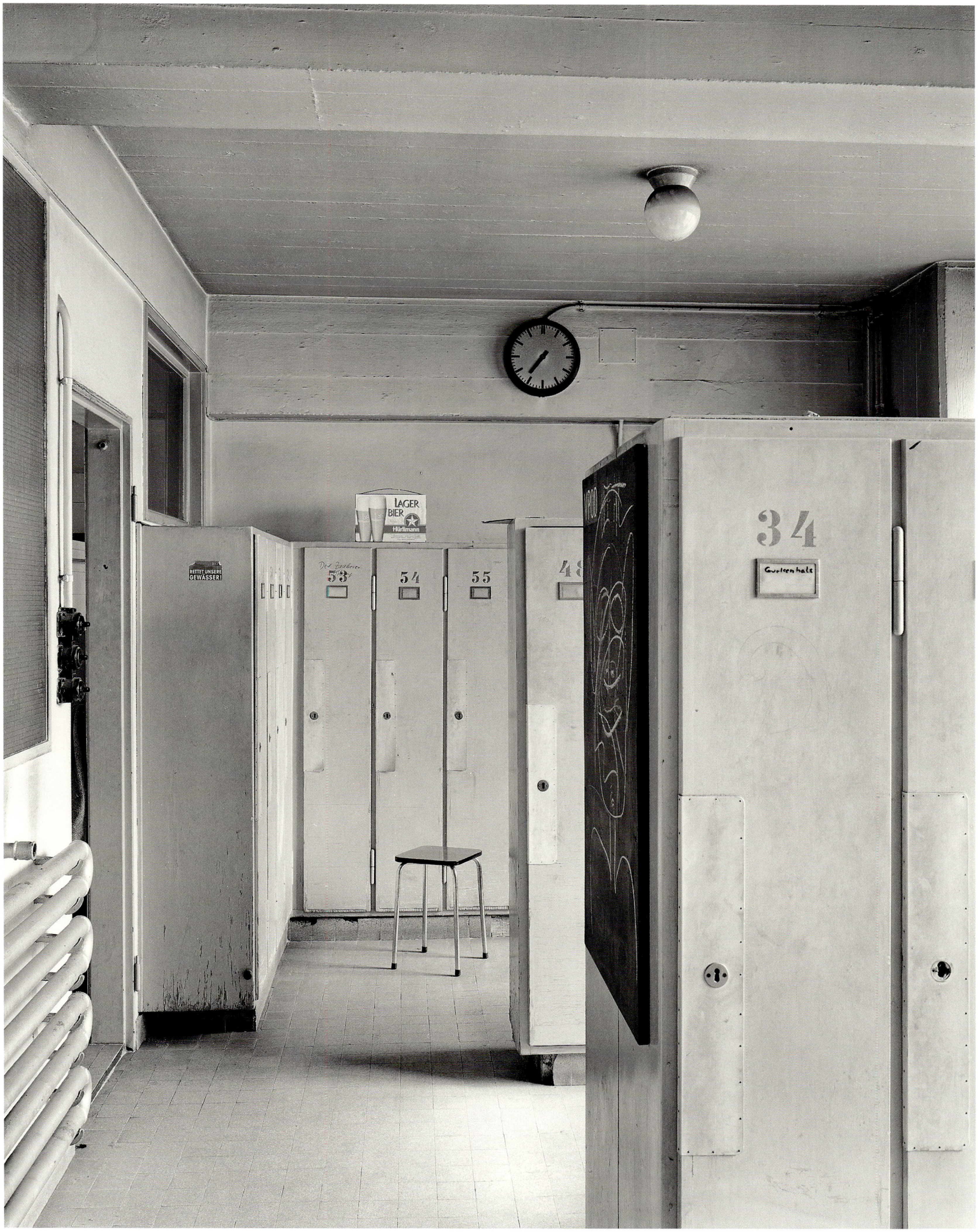
RETTET UNSERE GEWÄSSER!
LAGER BIER
Hürlimann
53
54
55
34
Gurkenhals

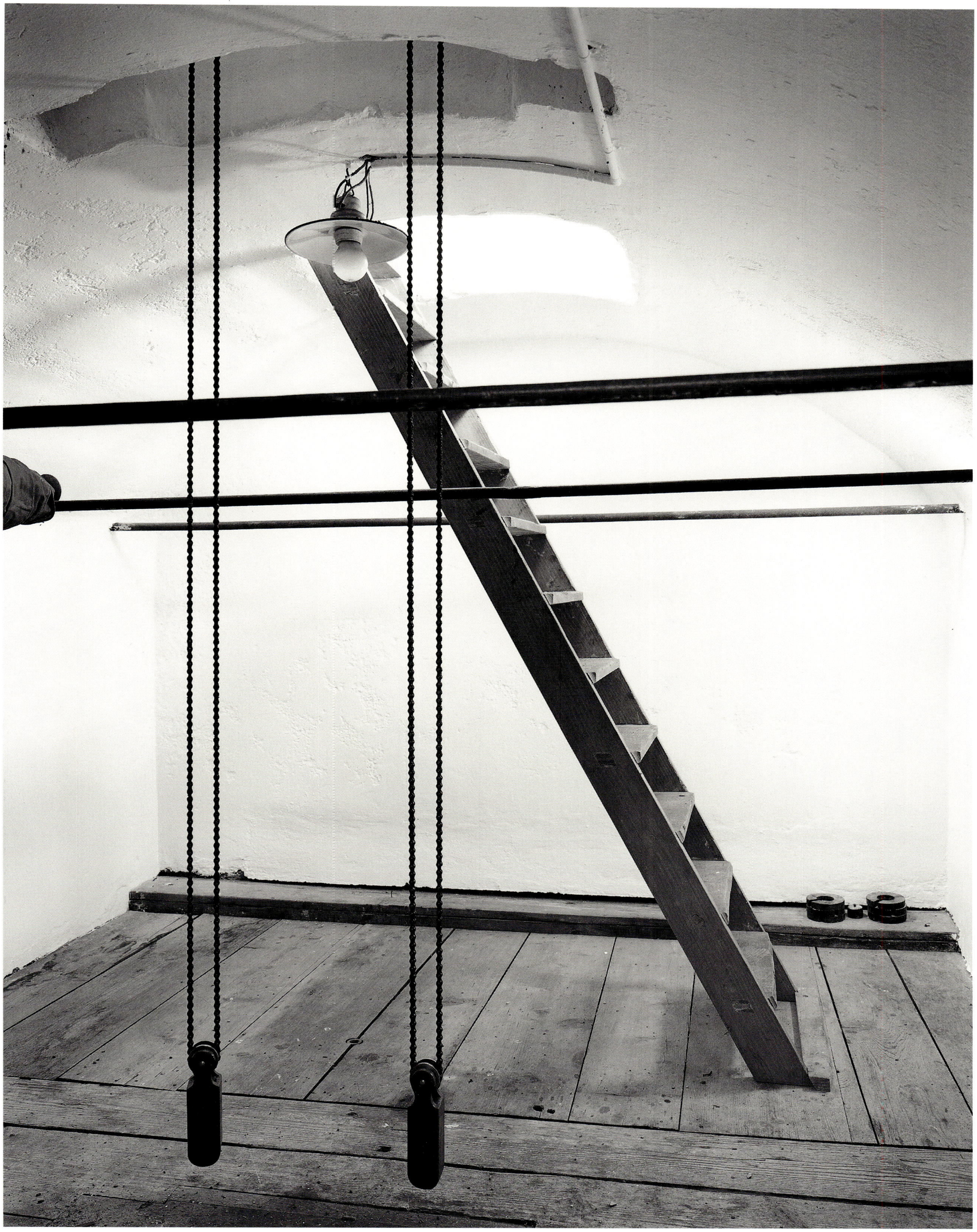

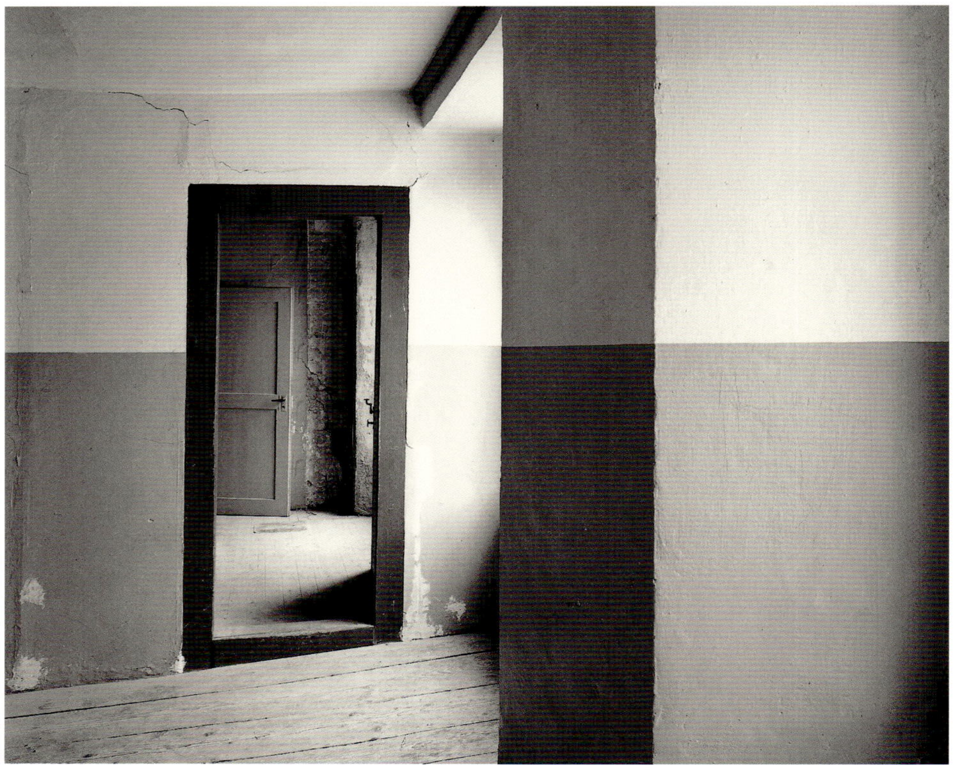

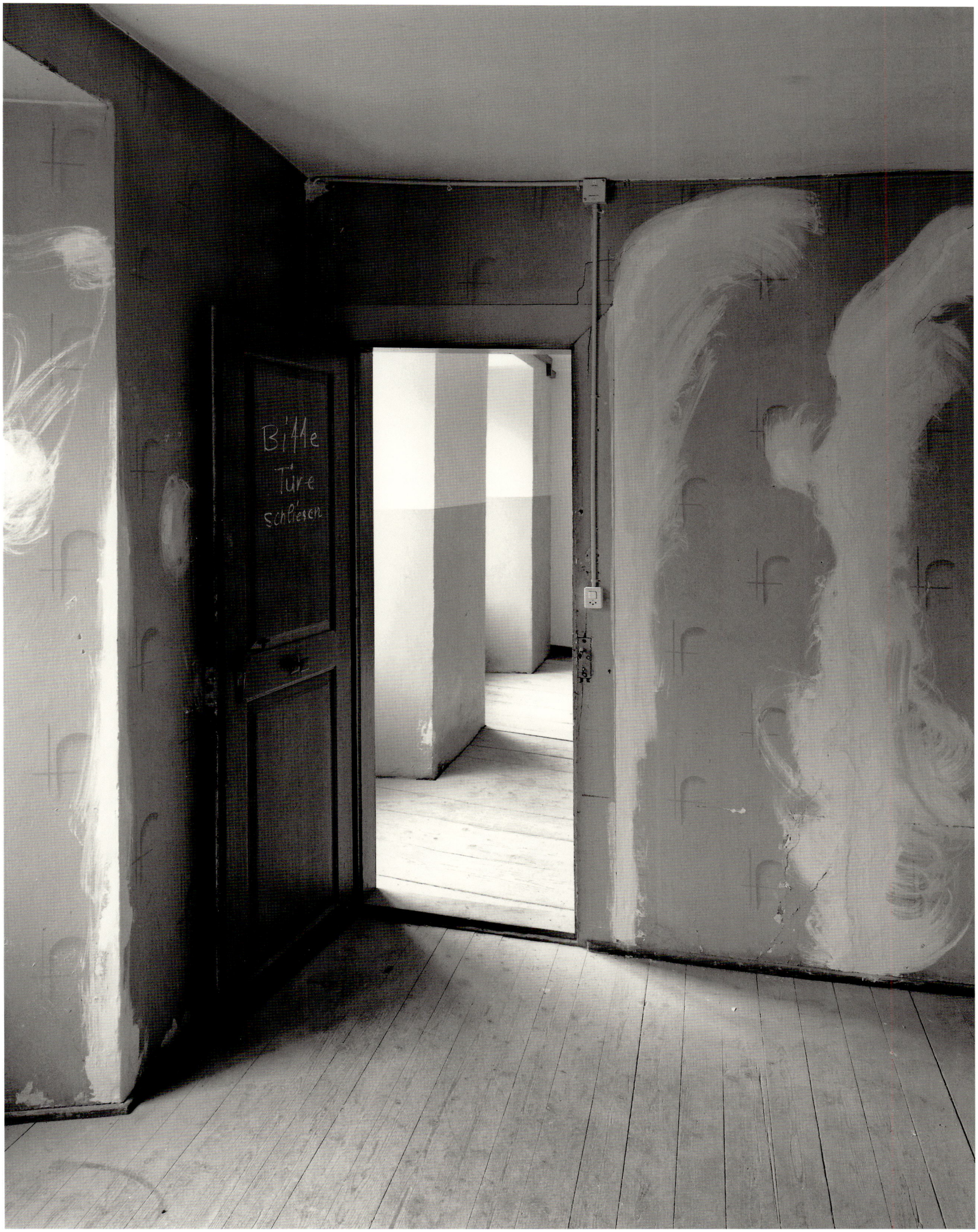
Bitte
Türe
schliesen

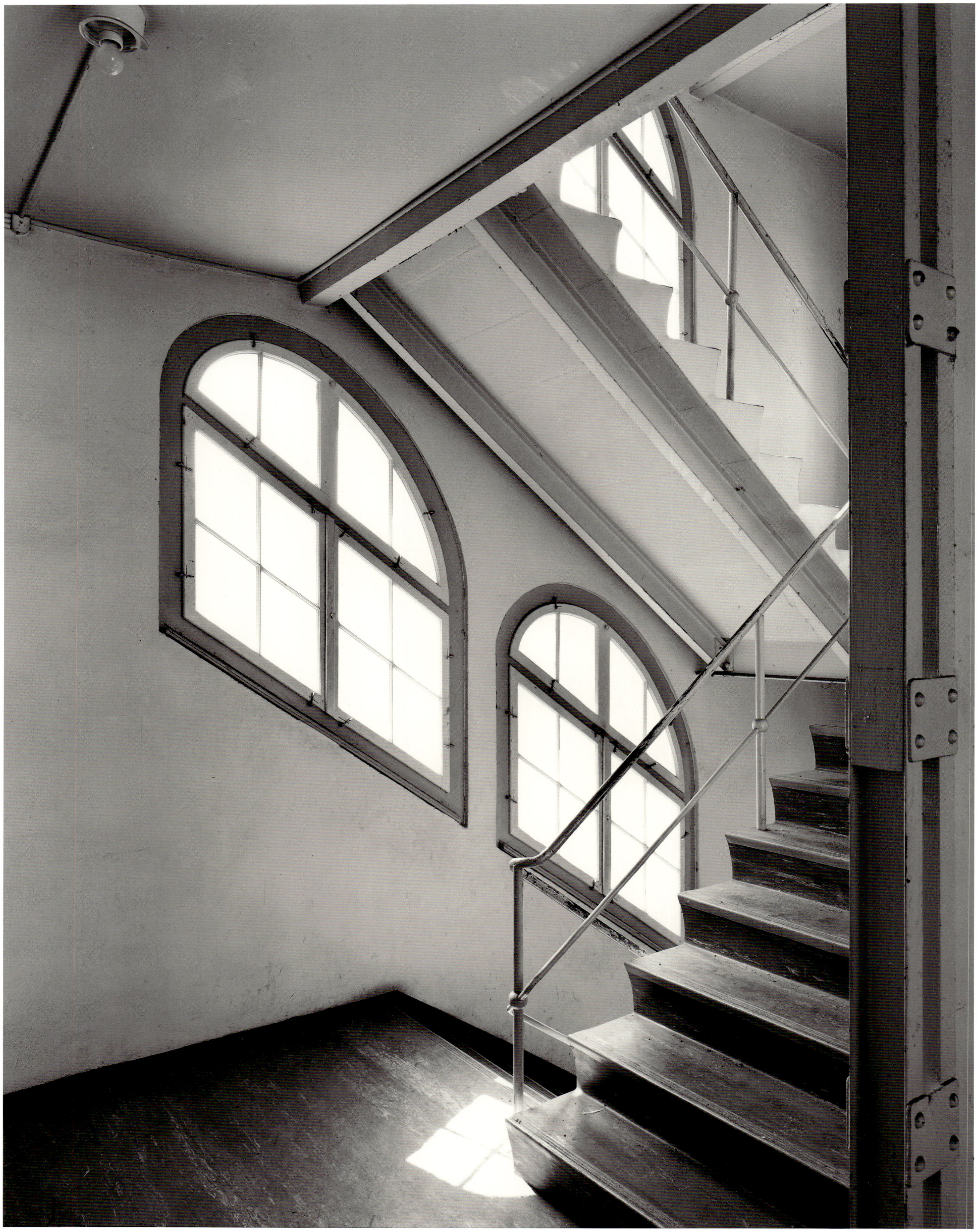

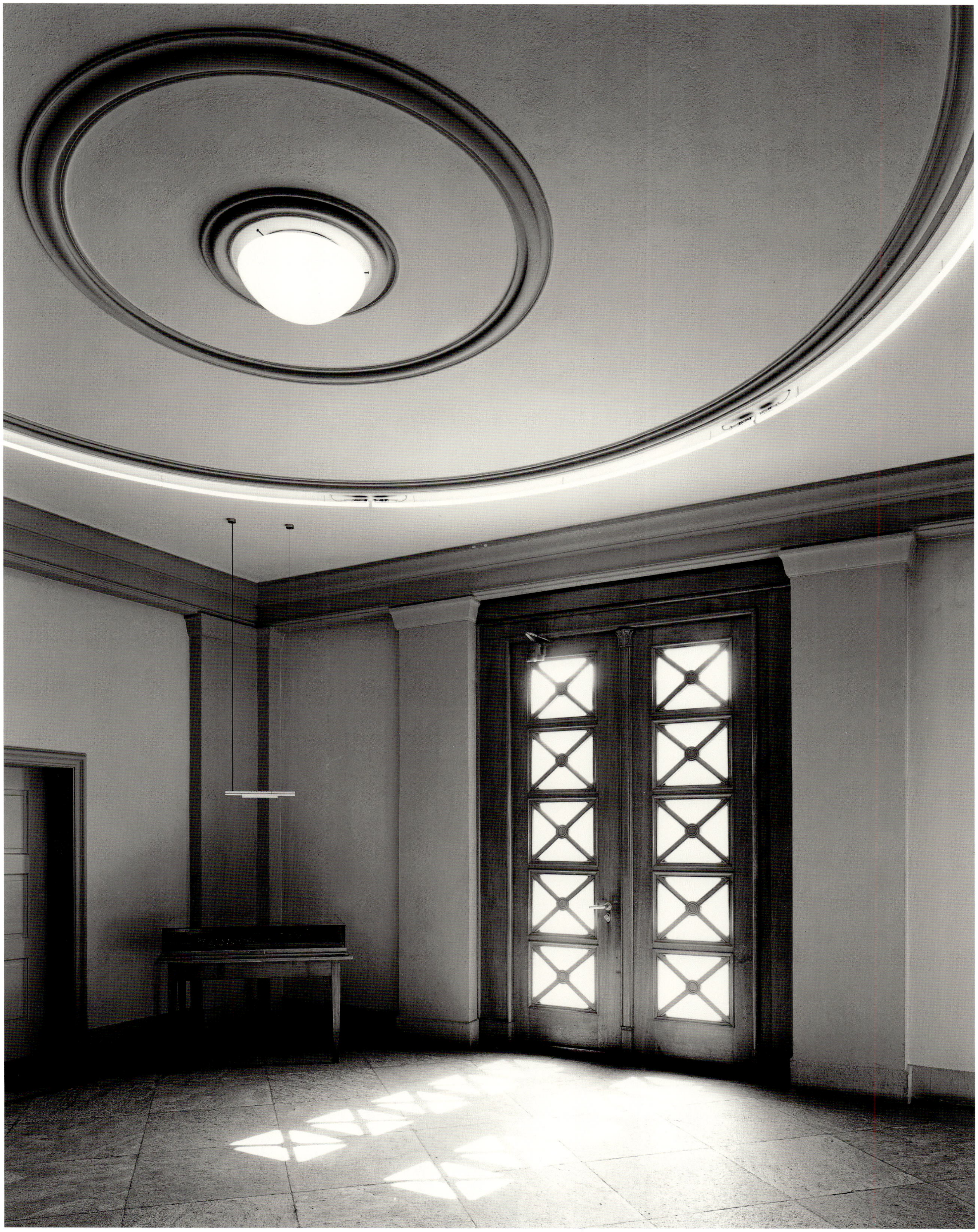

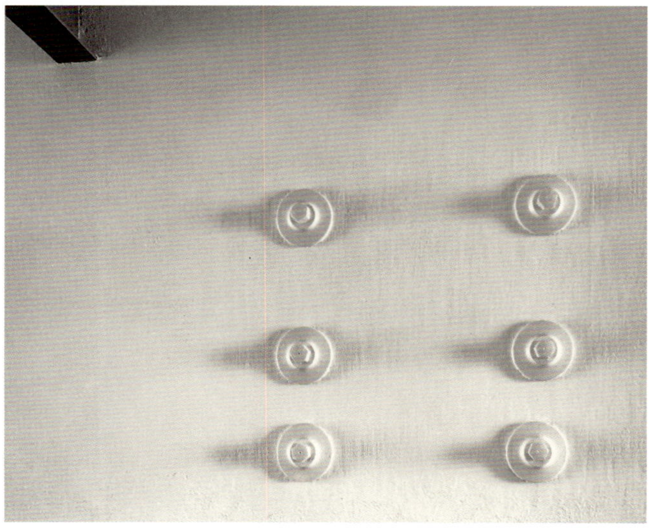

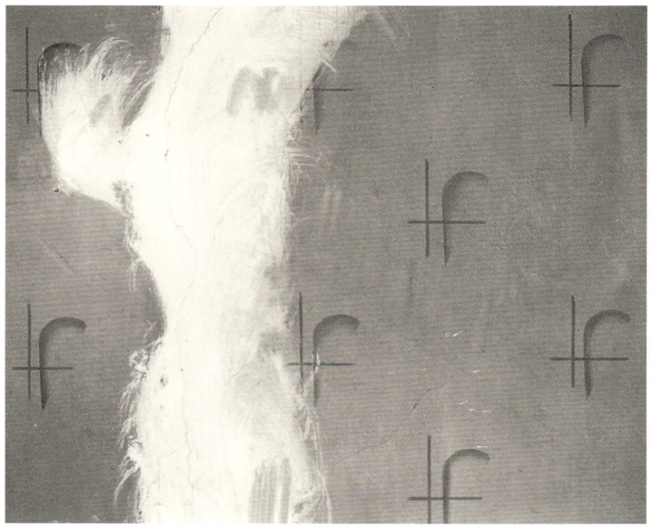

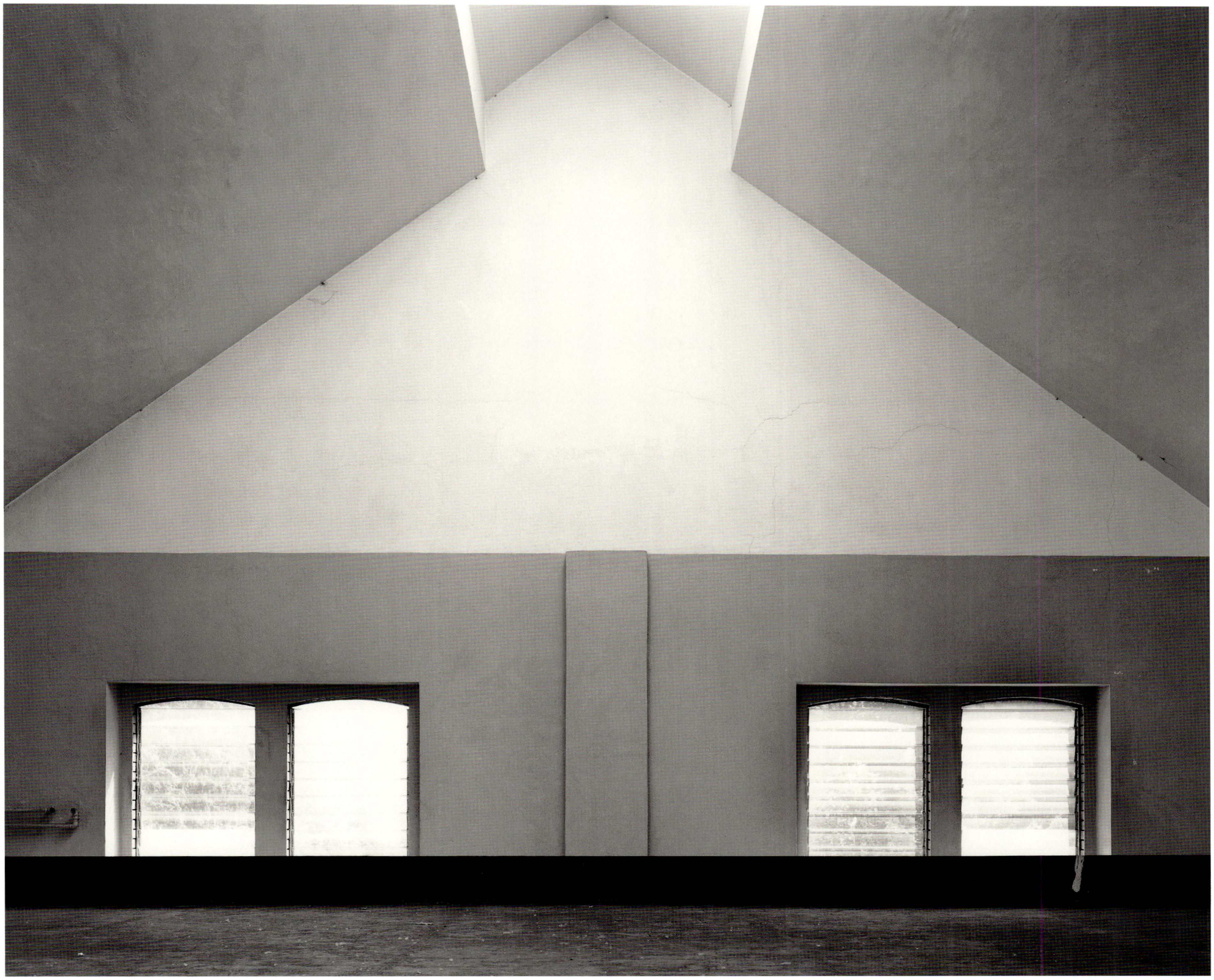

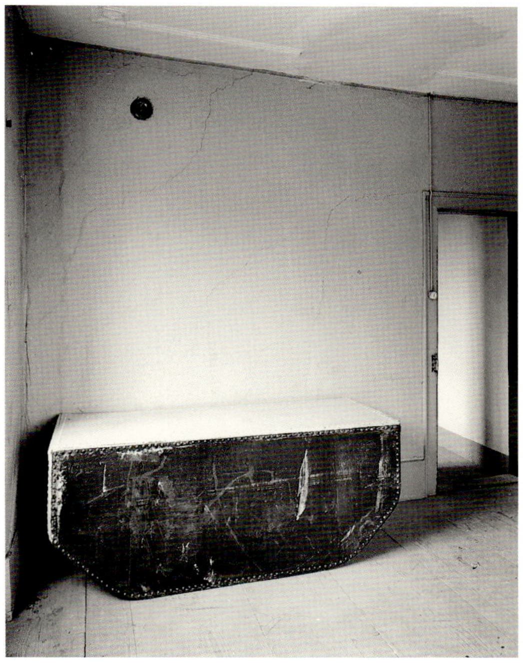

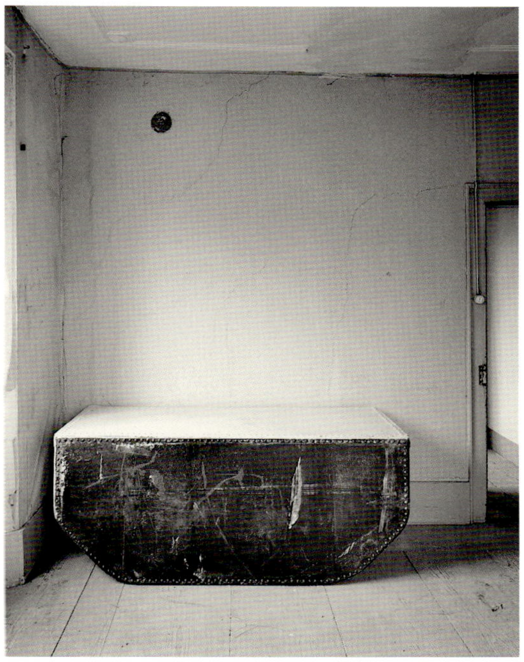

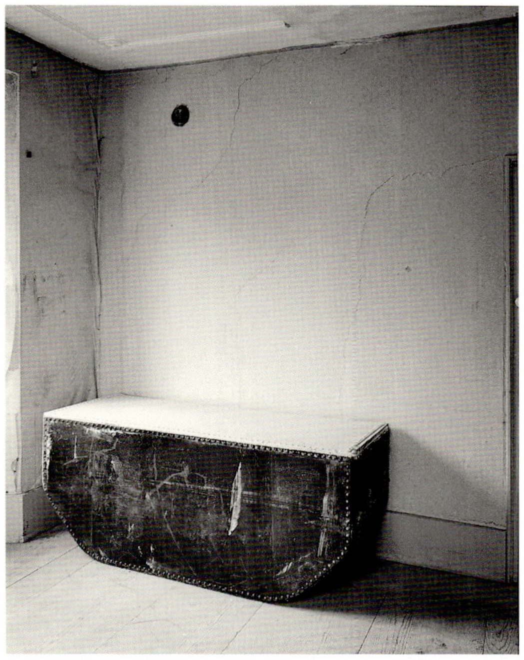

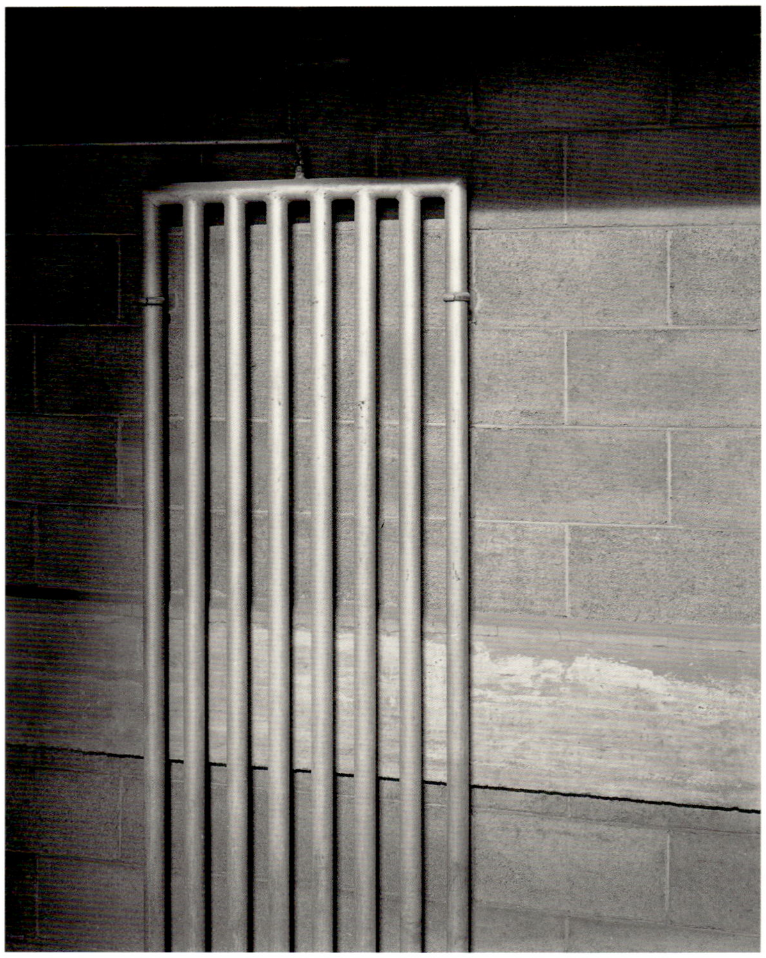

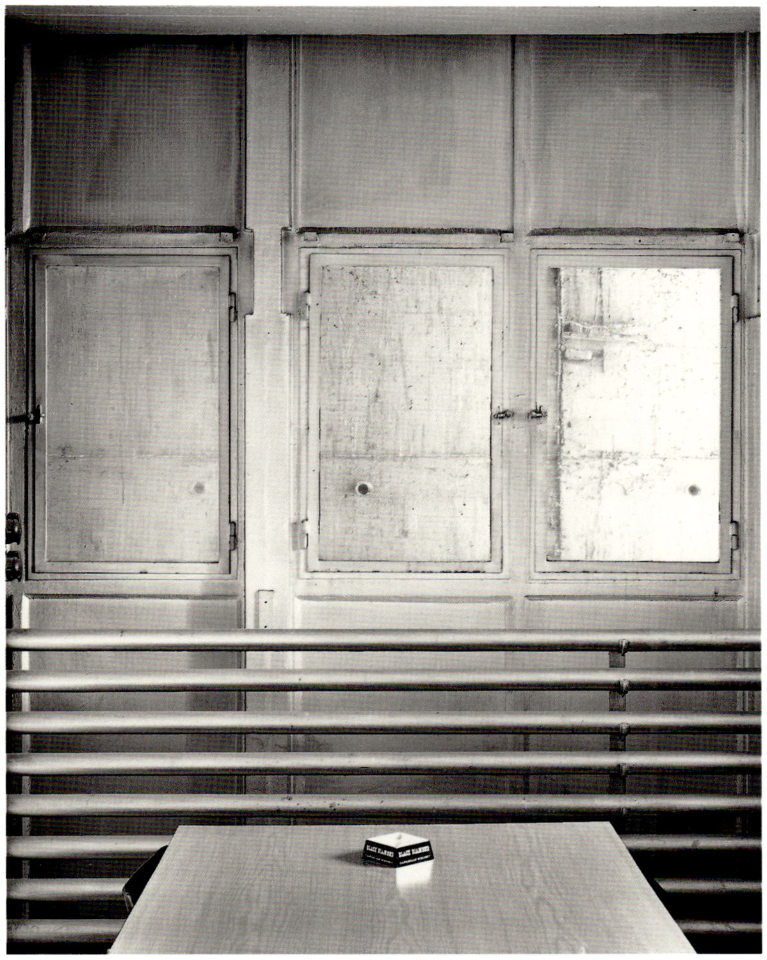

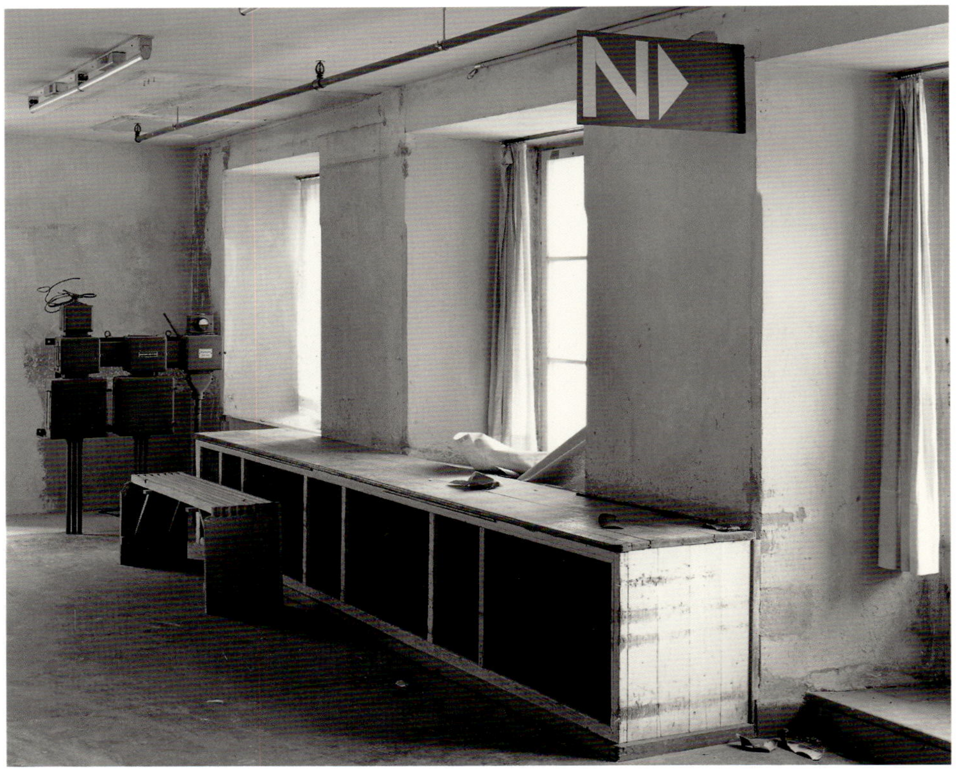
N

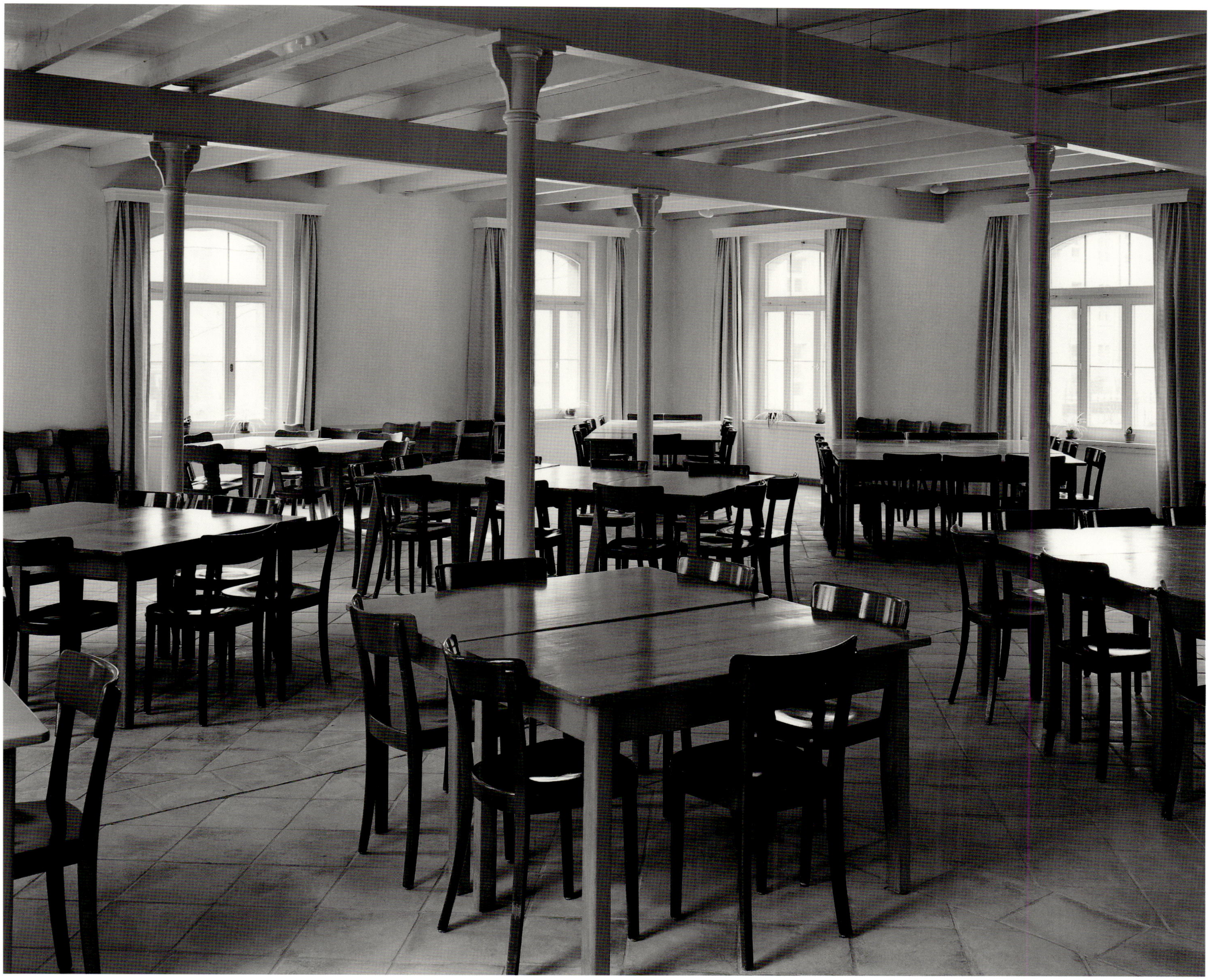

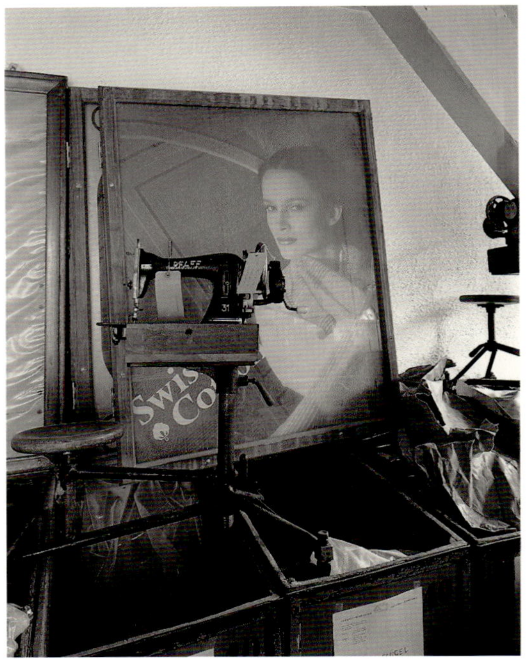

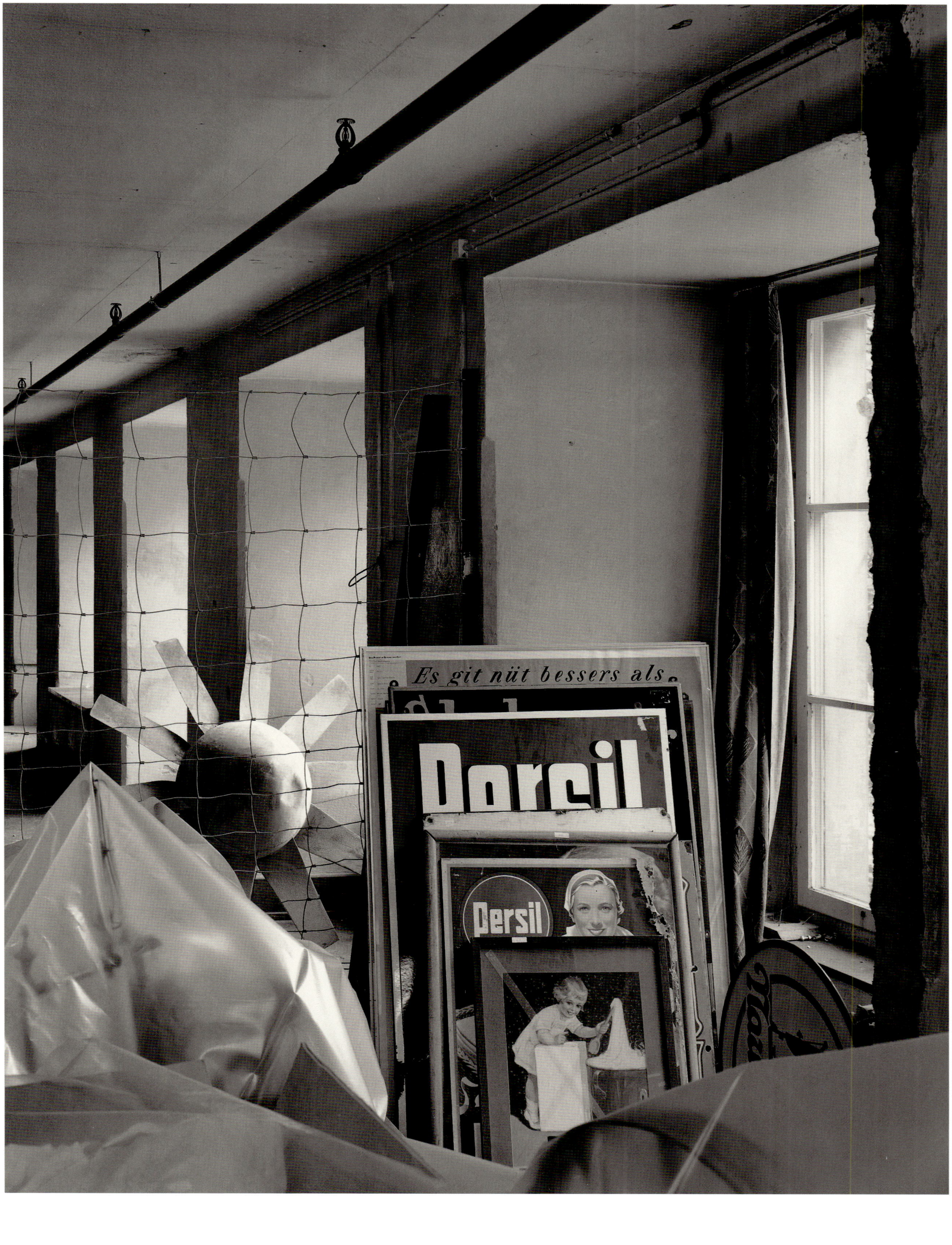
Es git nüt bessers als
Persil
Persil

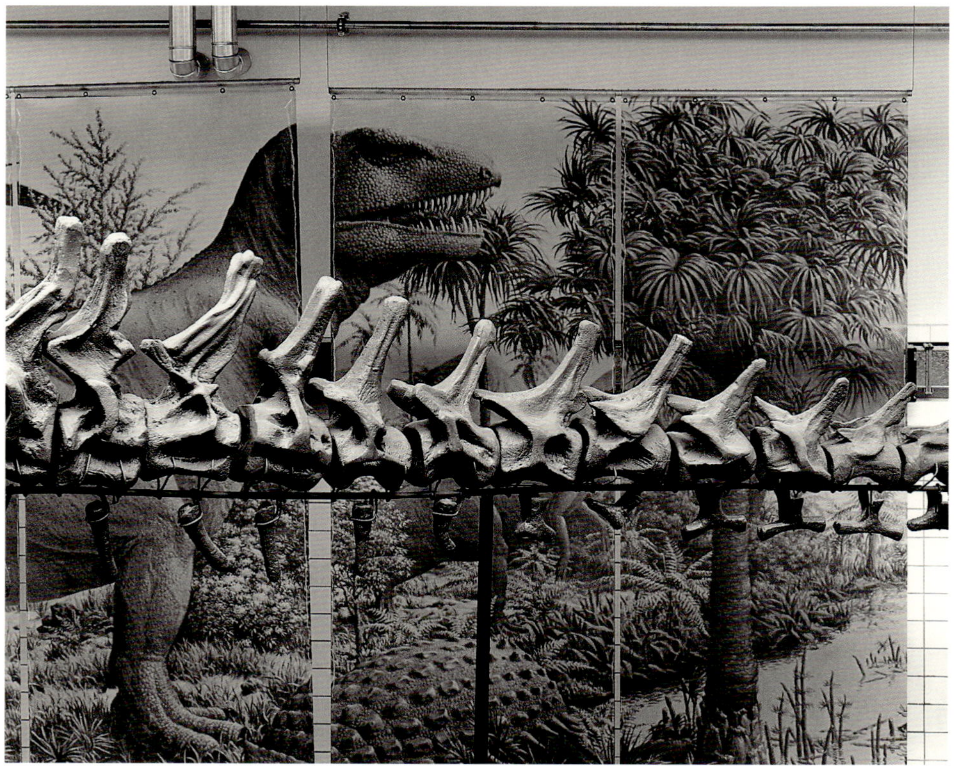

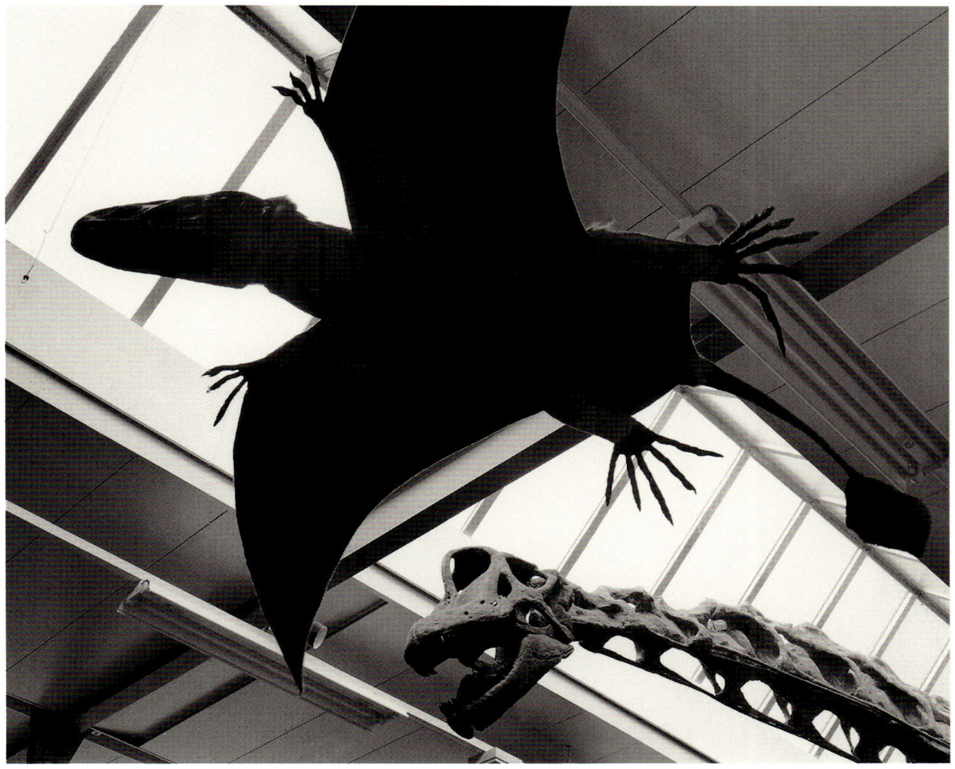

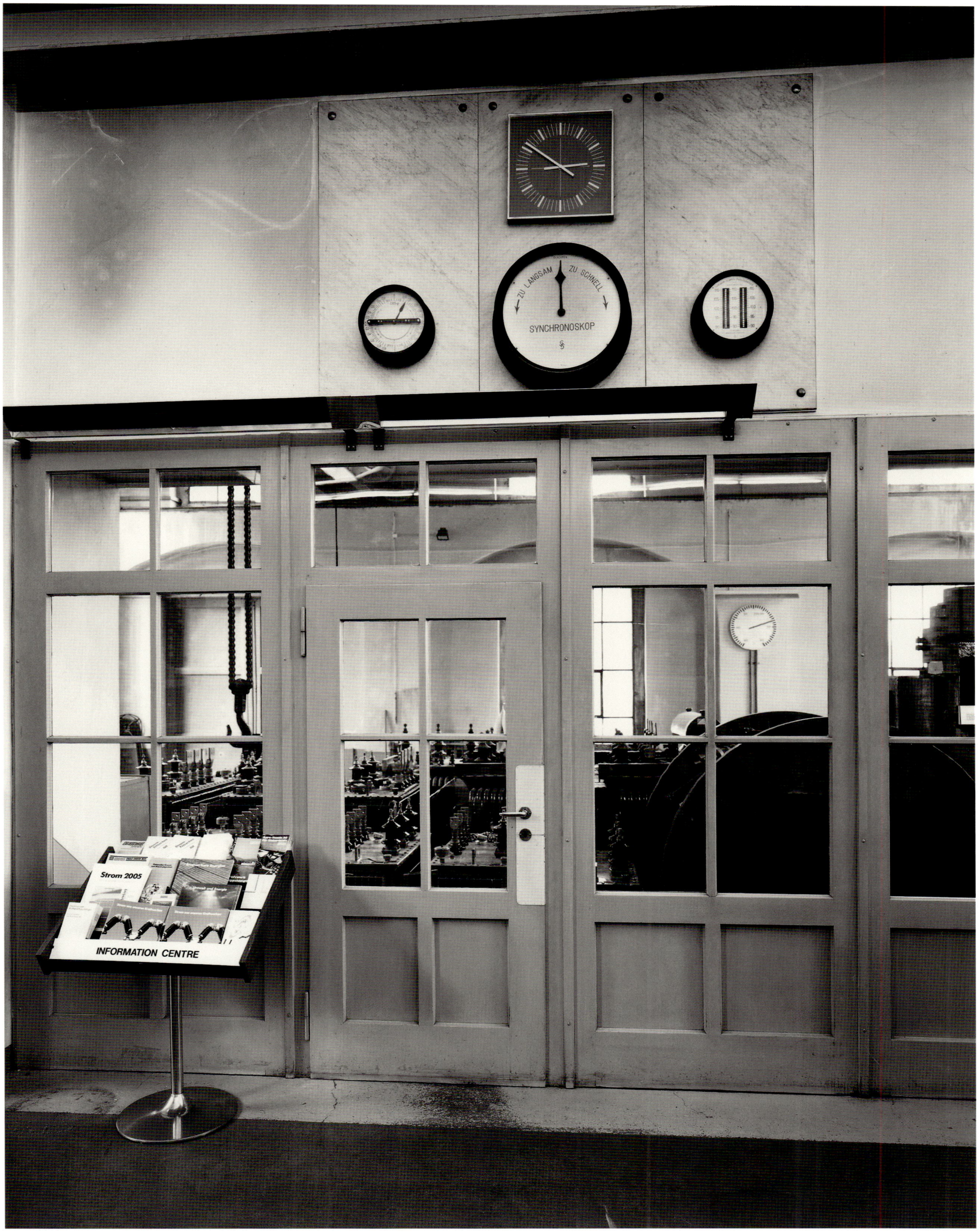
ZU LANGSAM
ZU SCHNELL
SYNCHRONOSKOP
Strom 2005
INFORMATION CENTRE

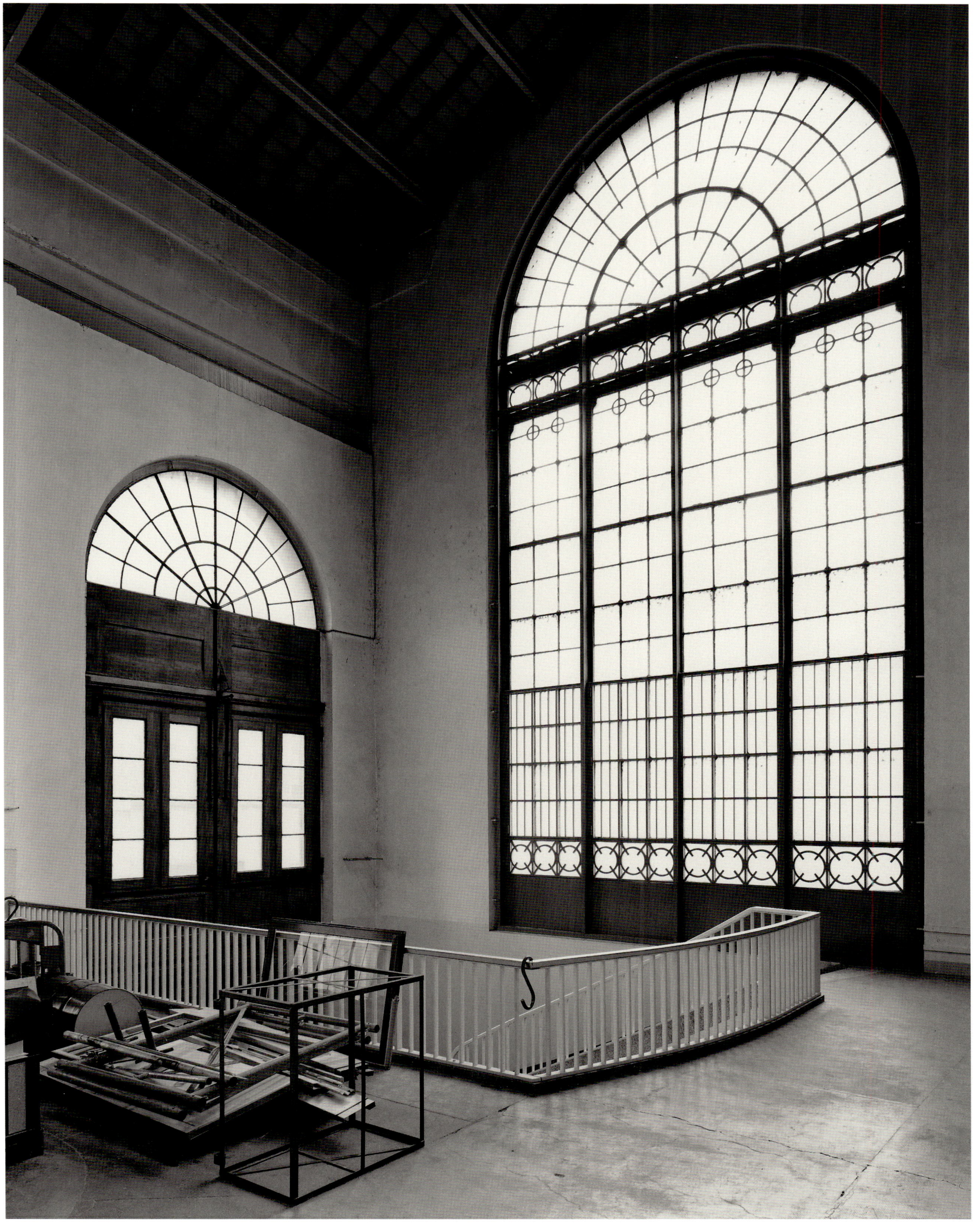

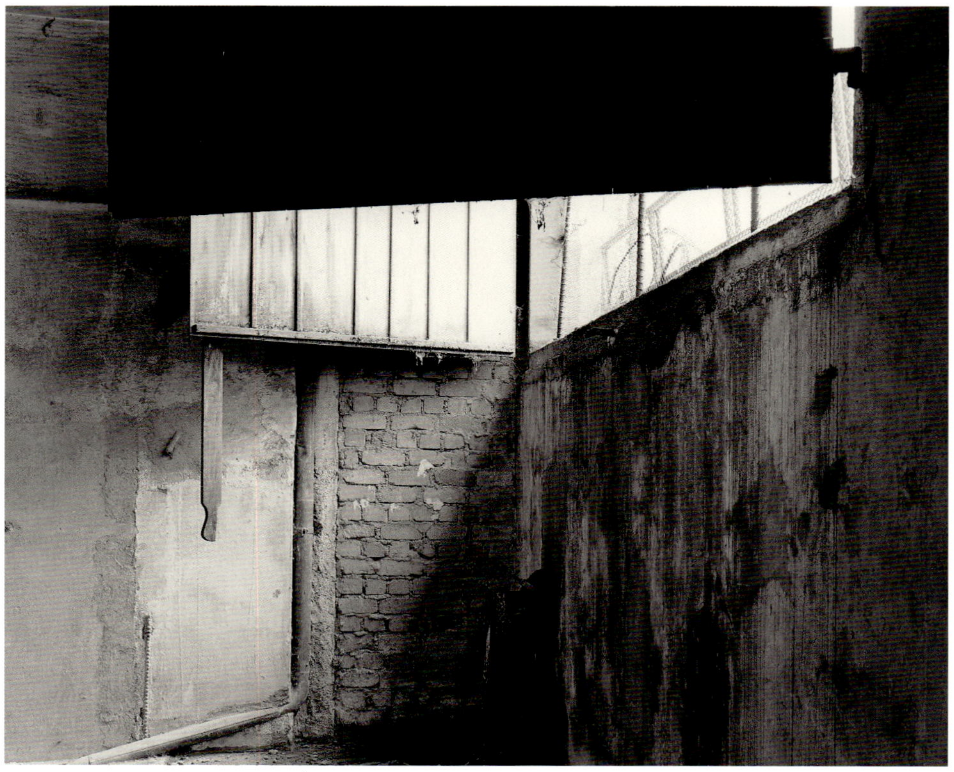

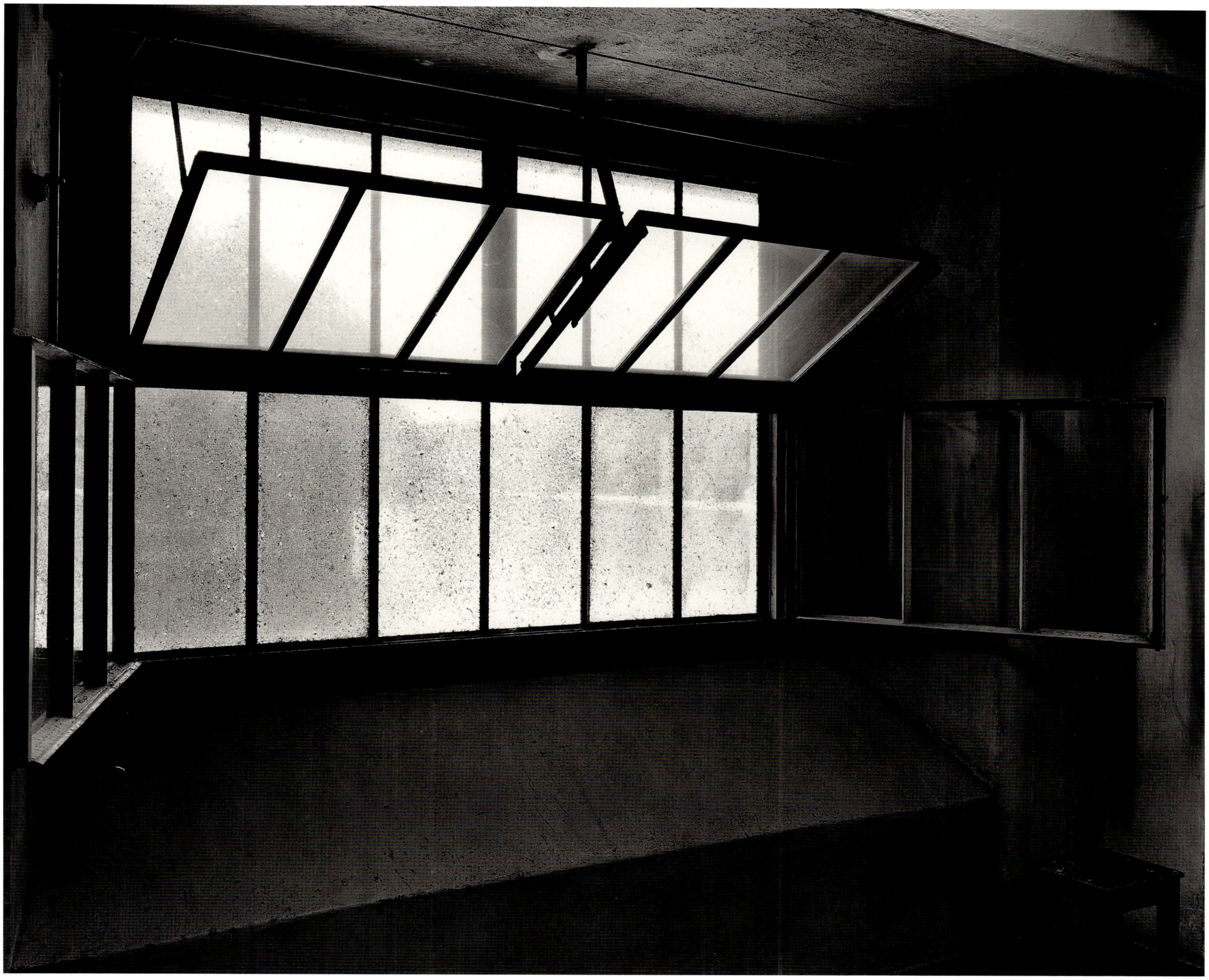

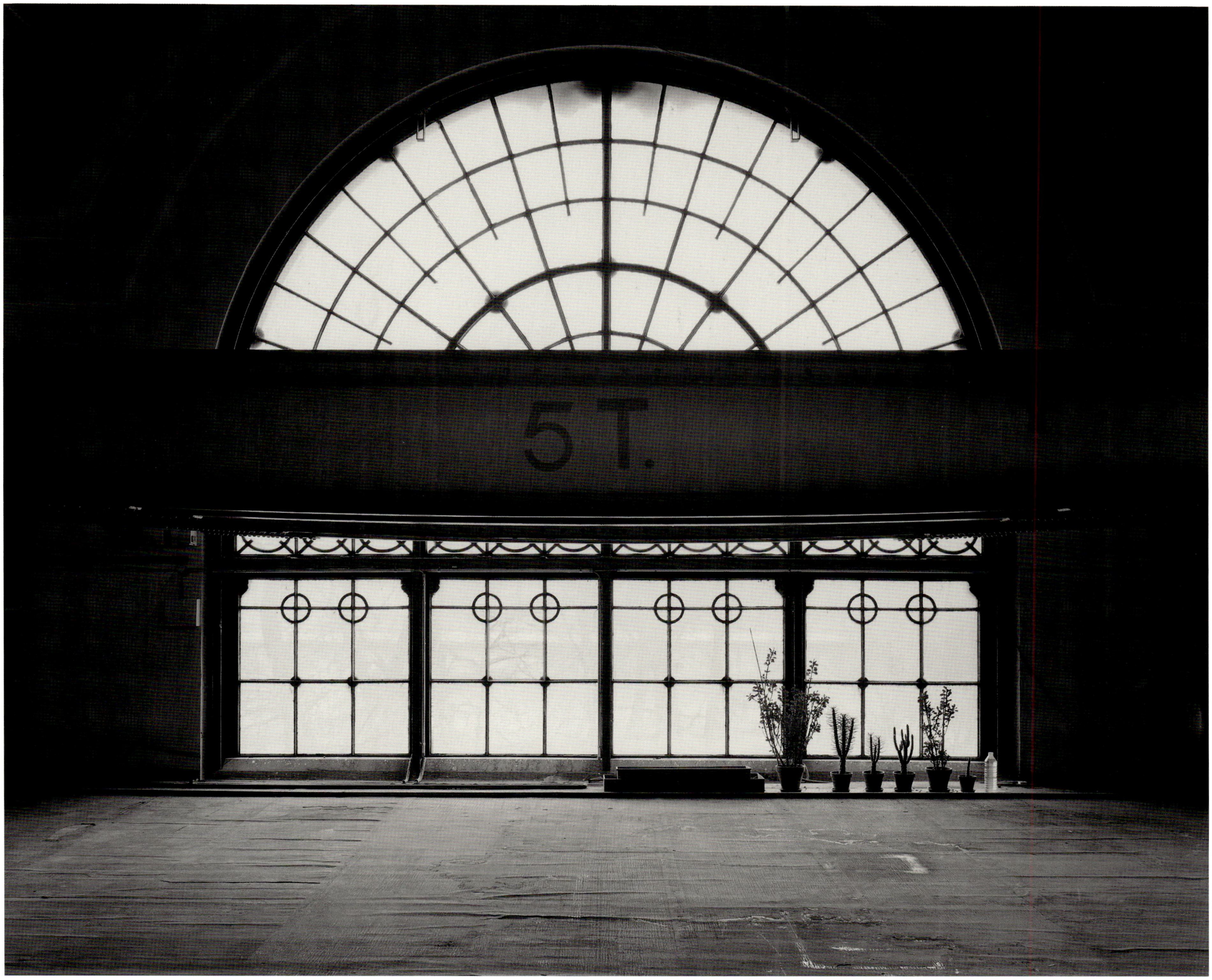
5T.

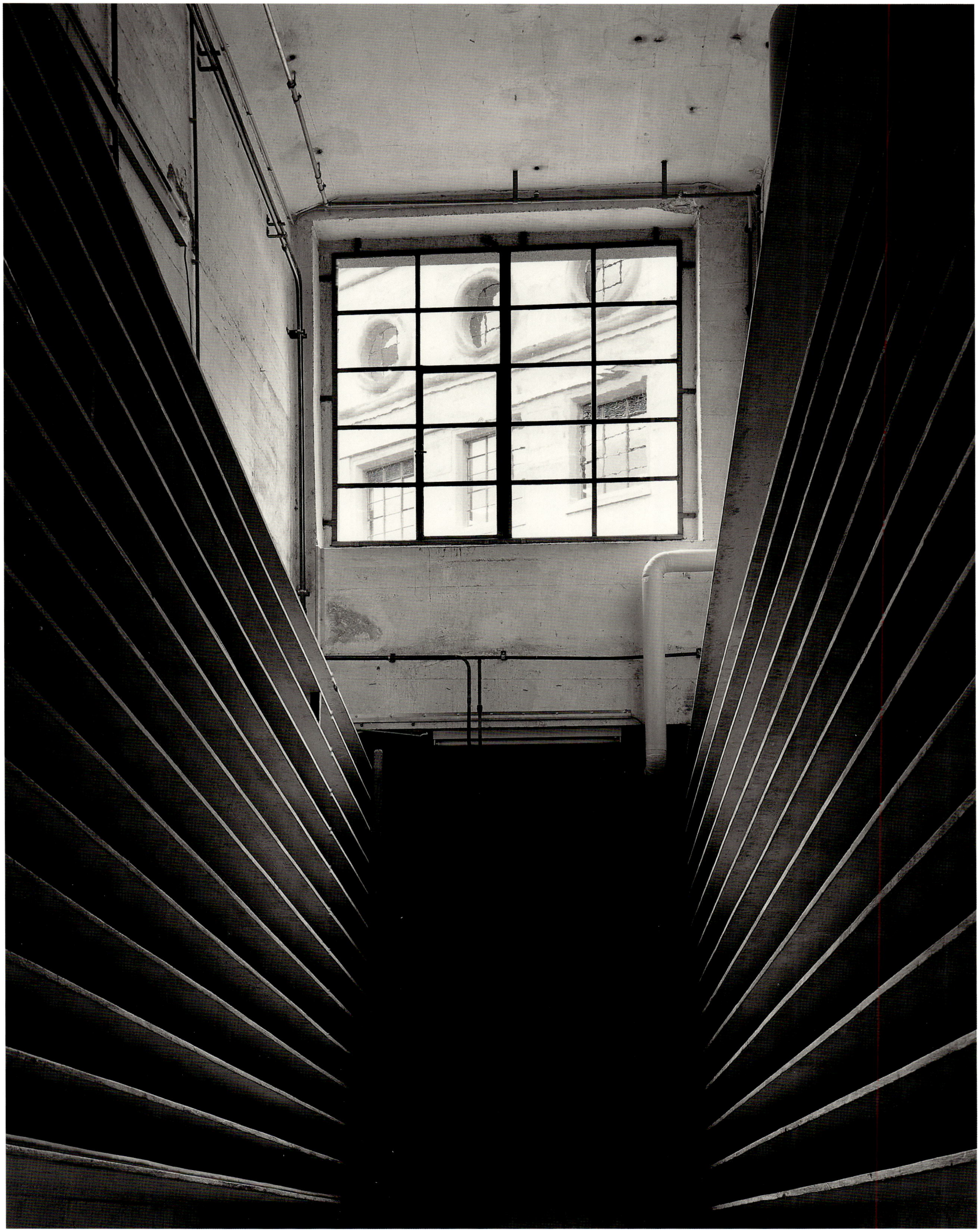

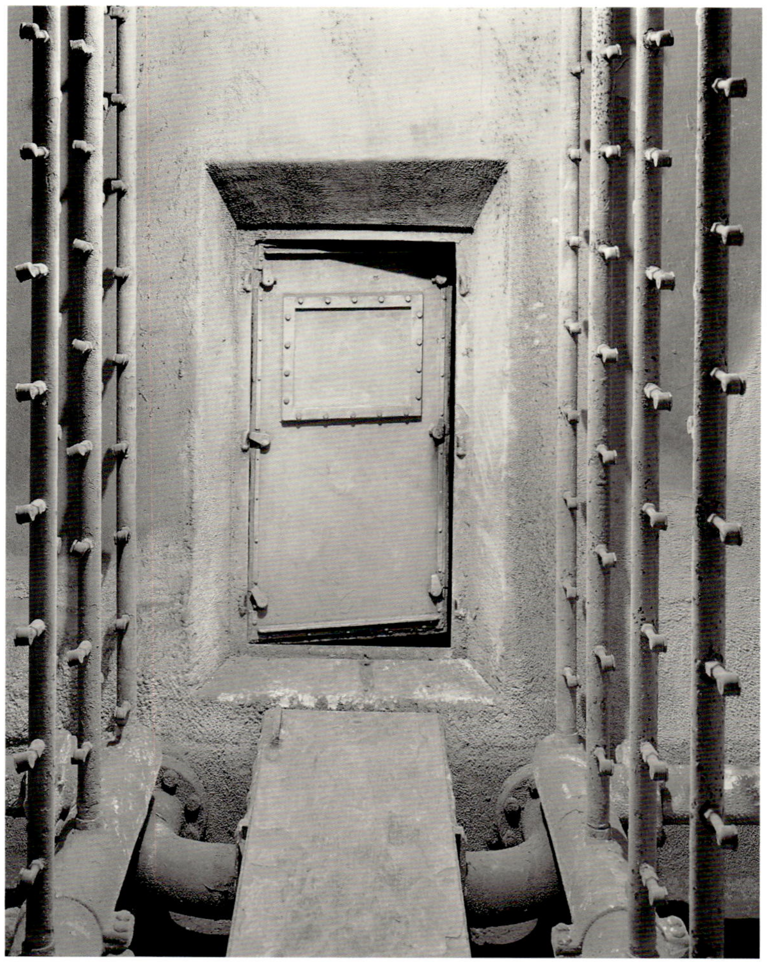

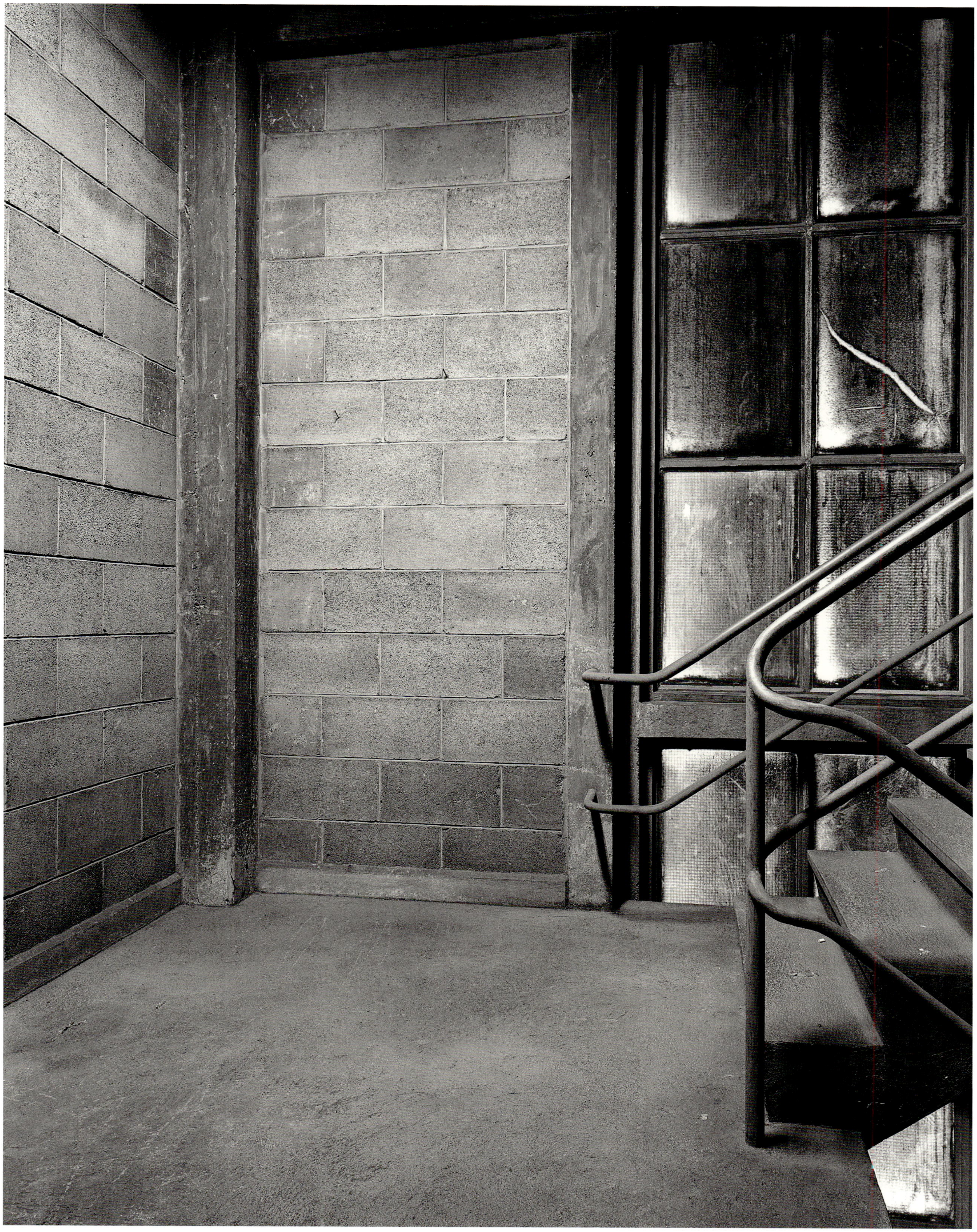

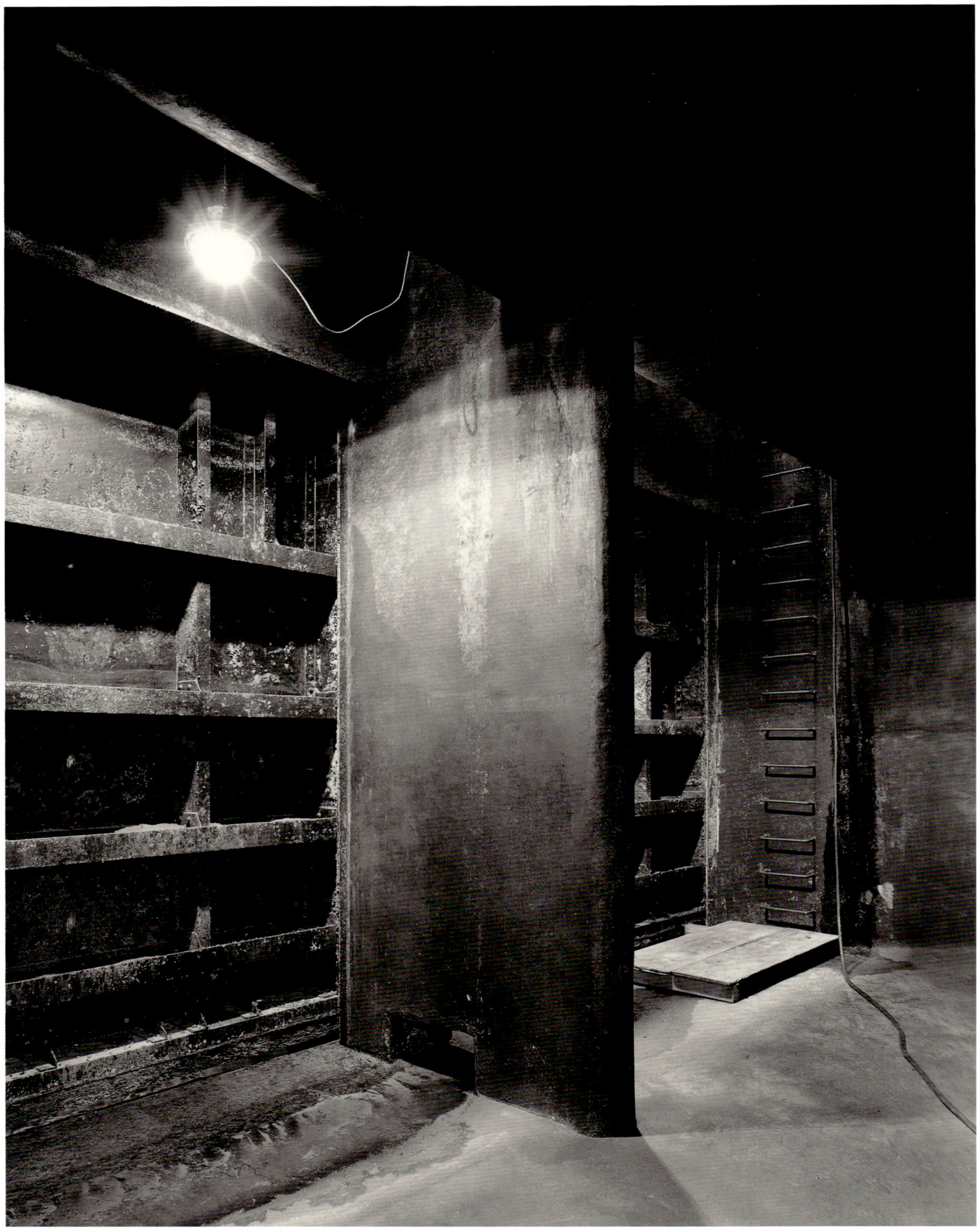

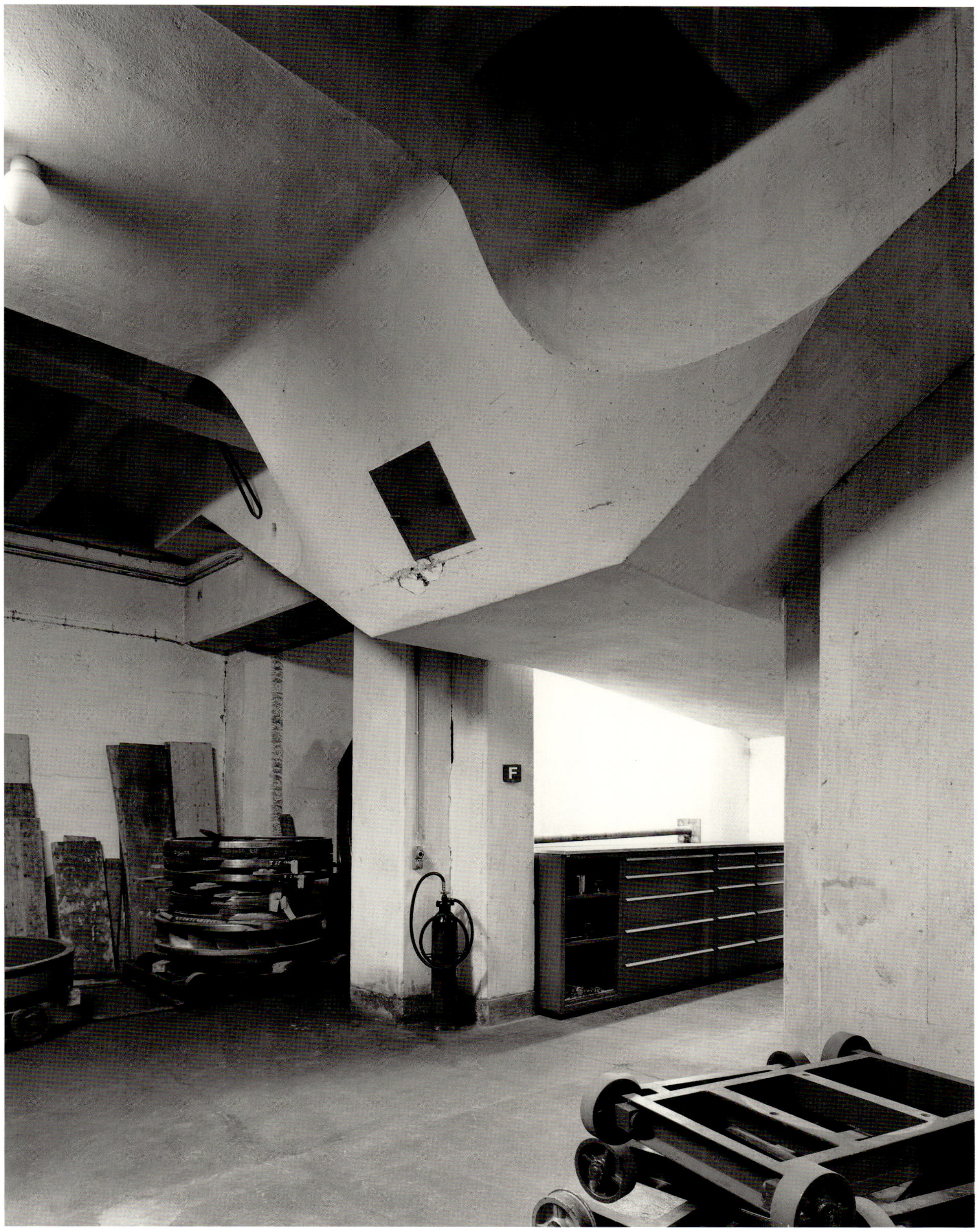
F

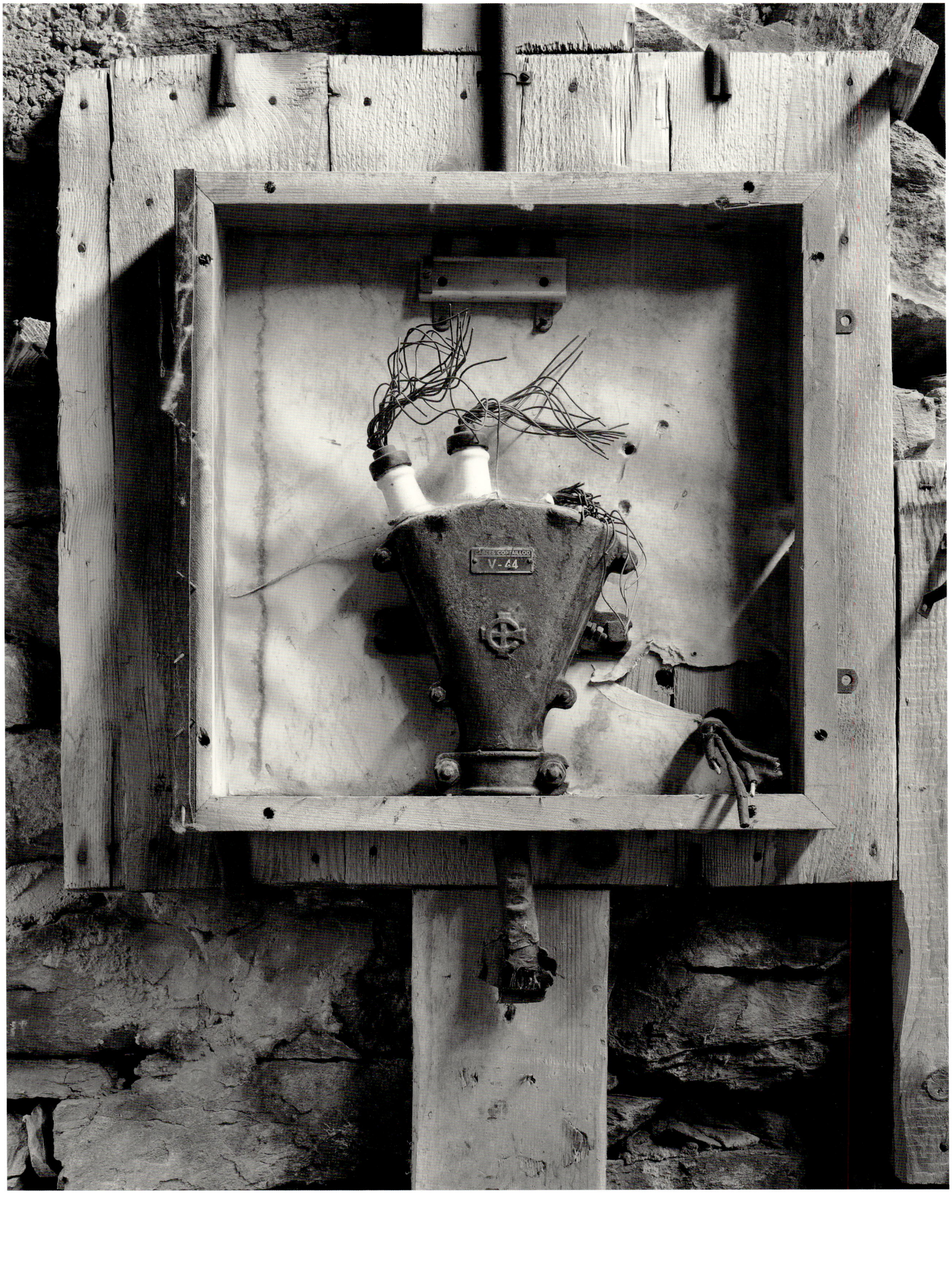
CABLES CORTAILLOD
V-44

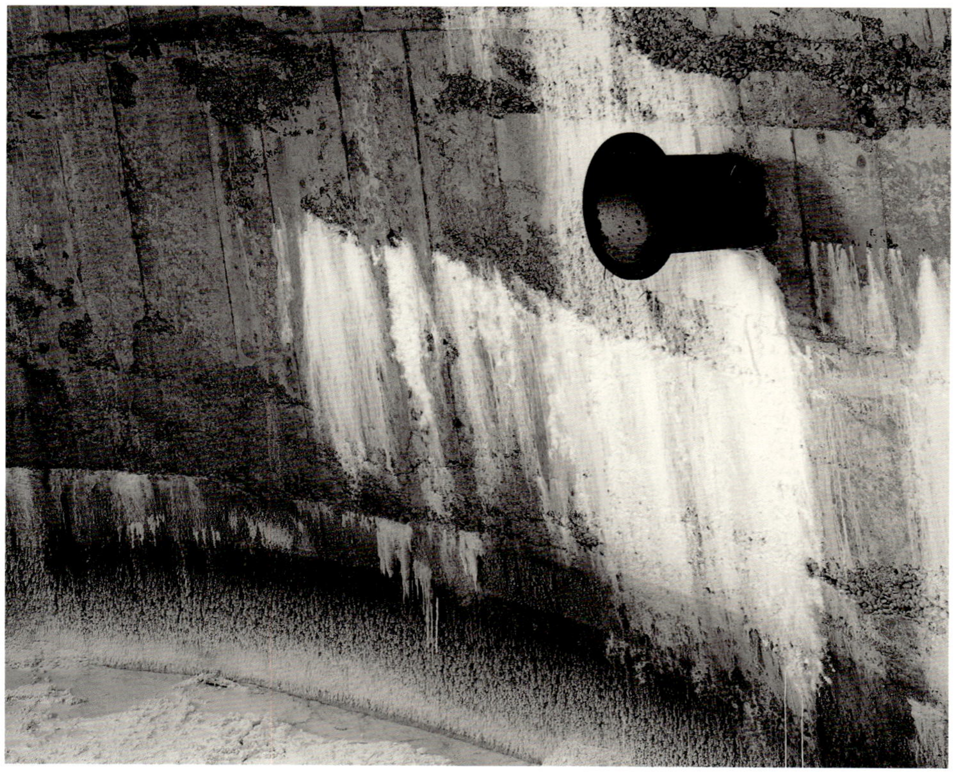

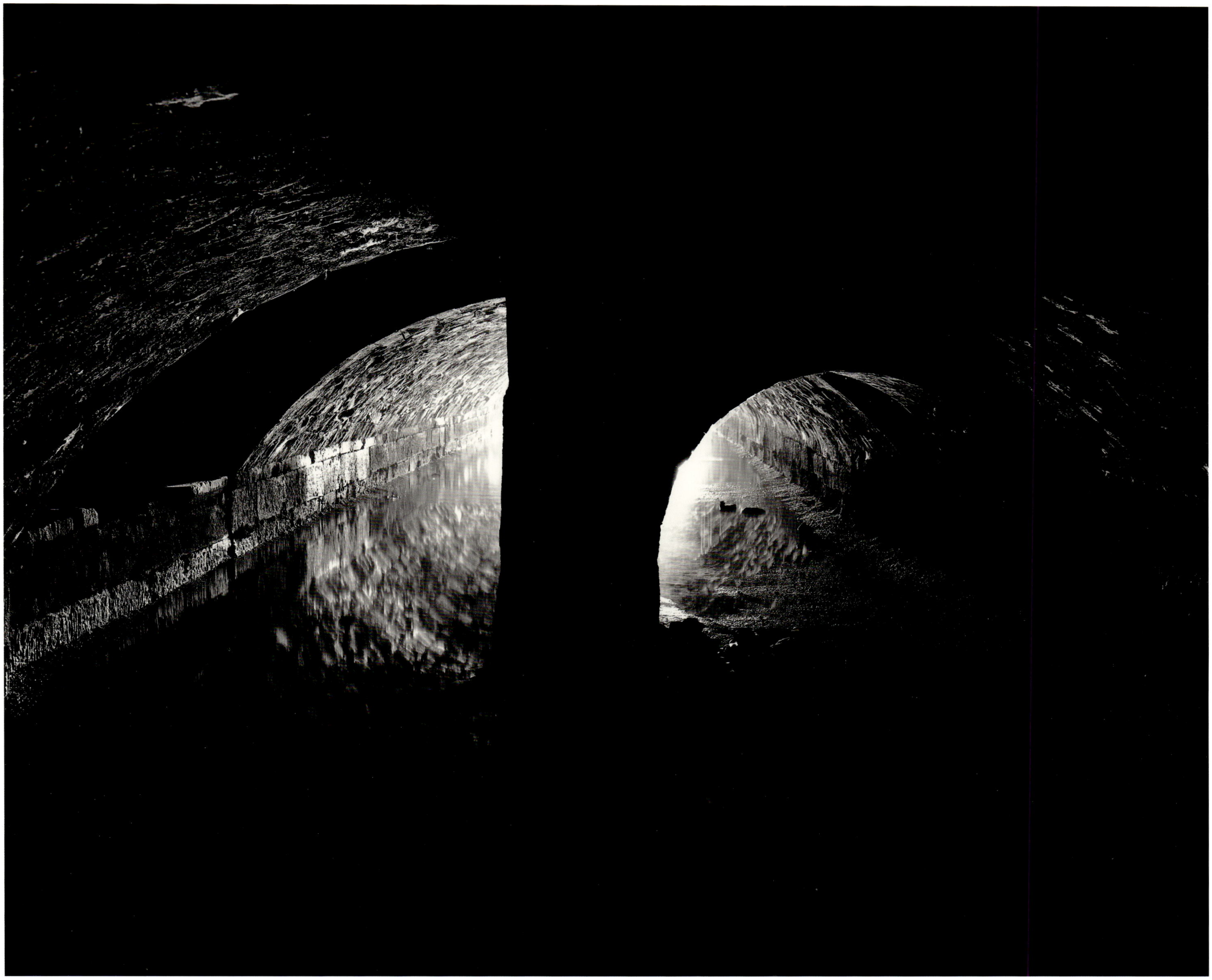

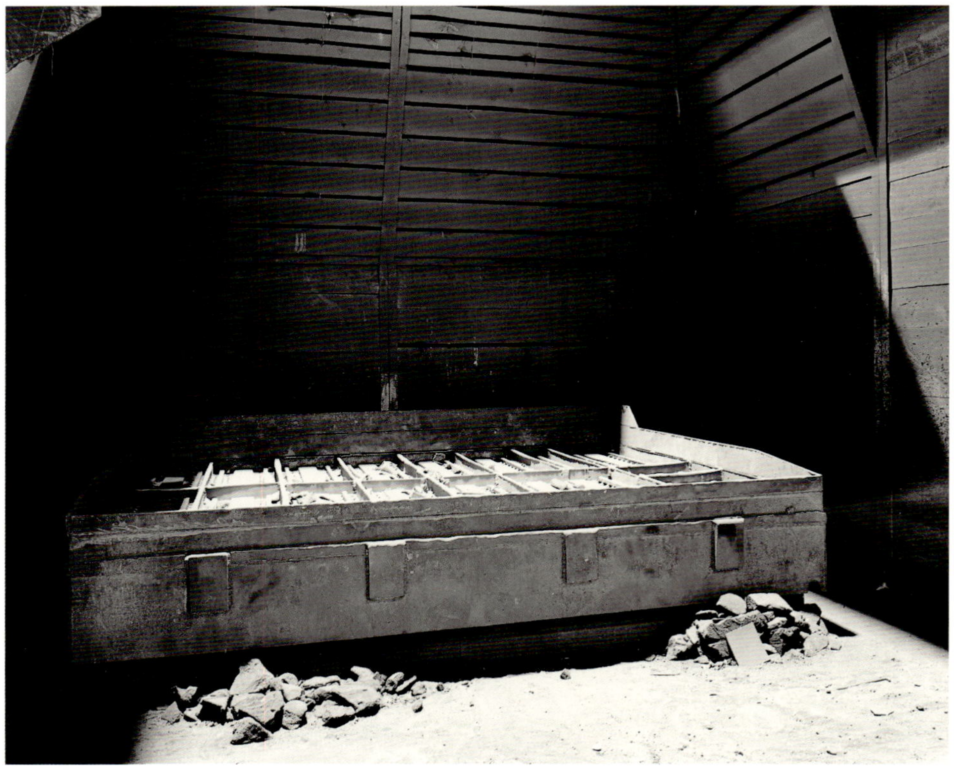

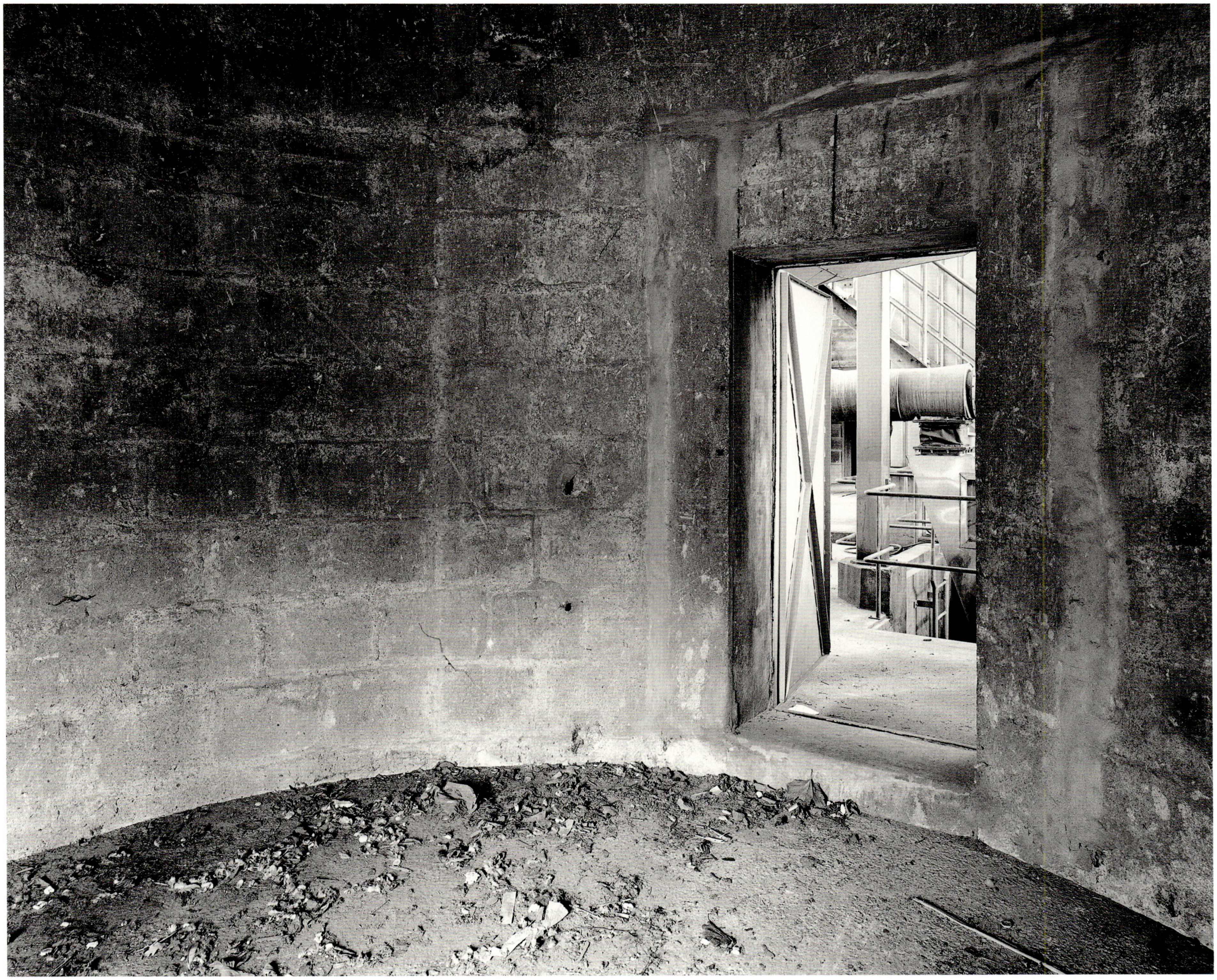

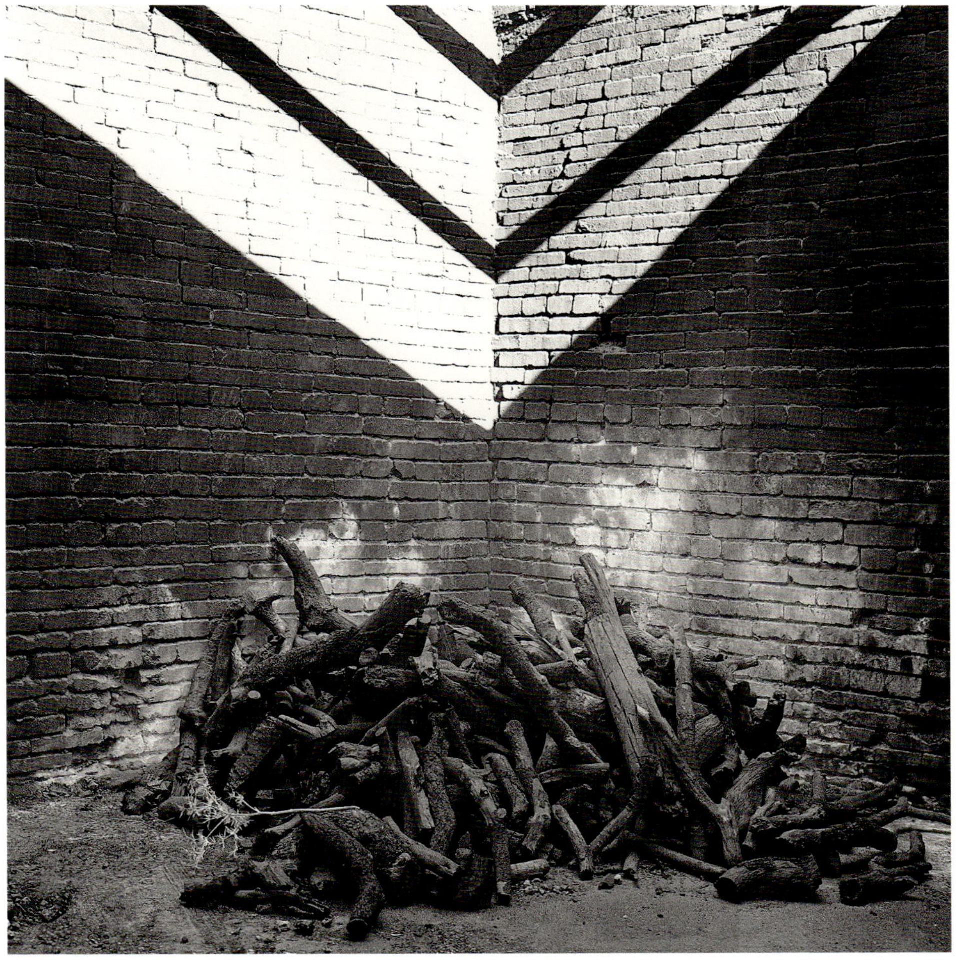

List of Plates

Unless stated otherwise, all photographs have been taken in Switzerland.

Page 42
Generator
Hydroelectric power station, Augst-Whylen
Whylen, Germany, 1992
In 1912 a twin power plant was completed on the Rhine extending over the German-Swiss frontier between Whylen and Augst, the powerstation on each bank being equipped by German and Swiss industries respectively.

Page 43
Chemicals tank in Oberwinterthur works
Machine and metalworking industry, Sulzer Ltd
Winterthur, 1991
Welding and chemicals: with growing diversification, heavy industry entered new business fields—in the case of Sulzer, for example, chemical separation technology.

Page 44
Water turbine: spiral casing
Hydroelectric power station, Hauterive (FEW)
Hauterive, 1992
When the Second World War broke out, electrification was pushed ahead throughout Switzerland. The Hauterive power plant in the Canton of Freiburg, with three Charmilles Francis turbines, was completed in 1940.

Page 45
Switchbox group
Spinning mill, STA Unteraathal
Aathal, 1989
Stable air temperatures and humidities are a critical requirement in the spinning industry. This automatic switchgear for controlling the air-conditioning system at Unteraathal cotton spinning mill dates back to pre-electronic times.

Page 47
Cast iron pillar
Brewery, Feldschlösschen Rheinfelden
Rheinfelden, 1992
Auxiliary rooms in production plants were often austere—all the more surprising to discover their striking spatial and lighting effects, here in combination with an elegant cast iron pillar.

Page 48
Fermentation room
Brewery, Feldschlösschen Rheinfelden
Rheinfelden, 1992
Business premises often reflect company standards, the highest priority in a brewery being cleanliness. In 1991 the Feldschlösschen brewery therefore modernized its fermentation and storage rooms, dating back to 1890.

Page 49
Staircase
Brewery, Feldschlösschen Rheinfelden
Rheinfelden, 1992
Not only customers and business partners were received in appropriate style, but also company personnel. This art-nouveau staircase in the Feldschlösschen welfare building, erected in 1929, leads to the employee facilities.

Page 51
Handwheel valves
Brewery, BIWAG Uster
Uster, 1990
Freshly brewed beer storage requires extensive refrigeration systems. The subsequently lagged ammonia piping and valves in this Uster brewery were manually regulated.

Page 52
Mash tanks
Brewery, BIWAG Uster
Uster, 1990
While the copper fermentation tanks and steam engine (1897) have been preserved in this brewery as historical showpieces, facilities hidden in the lofts were removed to make room for reutilization.

Page 53
Thrust-bearing pedestal
Hydroelectric power station, Eglisau (NOK)
Rheinsfelden, 1991
The electromechanical equipment at Eglisau power station was supplied in 1919 by Escher Wyss Zurich, Bell Kriens and Brown Boveri Baden. Since then it has been generating power almost continuously day and night.

Page 55
Francis turbine
Spinning mill, STA Unteraathal
Aathal, 1990
Rising power demands in the spinning industry were met by replacing the old water wheels with turbines. The hydroelectric equipment in Unteraathal spinning mill power station, built 1898, was modernized in 1905 and 1944.

Page 57
Generator
Hydroelectric power station, Wynau I (EWW)
Wynau, 1991
Together with Ruppoldingen, Wynau was one of Switzerland's first large power stations. This detail of the generator access dates back to the renovations of 1929. In 1991 the plant was demolished to make way for a new power station.

Page 58
Temperature sensor in Oberwinterthur works
Machine and metalworking industry, Sulzer Ltd
Winterthur, 1991
Adjoining the Oberwinterthur foundry was a heavy machine shop for products such as this giant marine diesel engine block.

Page 59
Turbine intake piping
Spinning mill, Bühler Kollbrunn
Zell, Tösstal, 1992
In 1939 this outer wall of the former waterwheel house—still with the original plastering and window—was pierced, to pipe water to the new Francis turbine supplied by Escher Wyss, Zurich.

Page 60
Fermentation tanks
Brewery, Feldschlösschen Rheinfelden
Rheinfelden, 1992
Wherever possible, breweries were built on sloping ground to allow for underground storage cellars. These Feldschlösschen brewery fermentation and storage cellars, dating back to 1890, were renovated in 1991.

Page 61
Fermentation tanks
Brewery, Feldschlösschen Rheinfelden
Rheinfelden, 1992
Thanks to modern technology, large-scale excavation and construction work is now more cost-effective than in former times. This new fermentation and storage cellar for the Feldschlösschen brewery was completed in 1991.

Page 63
Rotary kiln drive
Refuse incineration plant, City of Basle
Basle, 1995
Sulzer drive mechanisms like this kept the Basle kilns turning to incinerate all solid or bulk waste materials whose fusion point did not exceed 800°C.

Page 64
Elevator doors
Machine-building and metal industry, Zellweger AG
Uster, 1990
The administration building of this factory was designed to give a modern impression—as shown by the lighting, floor and wall decor, as well as the pushbuttons and handles on the elevator doors, with their porthole-type windows.

Page 65
Crane hatchway
Hydroelectric power station, Küblis (BK)
Küblis, 1991
A crane running under the roof ridge, lowered its hook through a hatchway to hoist heavy loads into the powerhouse below. This Prättigau power station, dating back to 1922, was built in regional style.

Page 66
Power station landing
Hydroelectric power station, Wägital (NOK)
Siebnen, 1992
The architectural concept of Siebnen power station dates back to the Bräm brothers, who completed the building in 1925 with modern interiors and expressionistic facades.

Page 67
In-house generation plant
Hydroelectric power station, Küblis (BK)
Küblis, 1991
Power stations not only generate but also consume energy. To ensure independence from the grid, in-house generation is an essential requirement in all power stations.

Page 68
Changing rooms
Brewery, Feldschlösschen Rheinfelden
Rheinfelden, 1992
Factories are defined as "buildings where workers mass-produce goods by mechanical means." These changing rooms at the Feldschlösschen brewery illustrate one aspect of what this used to mean.

Page 69
Changing rooms
Refuse incineration plant, City of Basle
Basle, 1995
If changing rooms represent the development of social awareness in industry, this incineration plant, built in 1943, lags far behind the spacious Feldschlösschen brewery changing rooms dating back to 1929.

Page 71
Turicum factory clock weights
Machine-building and metal industry, Zellweger AG
Uster, 1990
After the industrial revolution, the rhythm of life was largely dictated by the factory clock. This Andelfingen weight-driven clock dating back to 1868 signalled the beginning and end of the working day, before watches became affordable for the masses.

Page 72
Stairwell rooms
Spinning mill, Neuthal spinning museum
Neuthal, Bäretswil, 1994
"Honour the calloused hands and the work-worn houses..." After 170 years of land-subsidence and labour, the stairwell beams and walls in the Neuthal spinning mill are well out off line.

Page 73
Master spinner's room
Spinning mill, Neuthal spinning museum
Neuthal, Bäretswil, 1994
Which master craftsman had the walls redecorated to his taste in this old spinning mill? Electric lighting was added later on, and the wall paintwork was restored when the mill became a museum.

Page 74
Staircase
Spinning mill, STA Flos Wetzikon
Wetzikon, 1990
The architect who added this imposing staircase tower in 1916 to the Flos I spinning mill, almost a century old, was none other than Johannes Meier. For years he was master architect to nearly all the industrialists in this region.

Page 75
Reception room
Hydroelectric power station, Eglisau (NOK)
Rheinsfelden, 1991
Judging by the wall pilasters, stucco ceiling and heavy panelled doors, visitors here might think themselves in the reception hall of an administration building. In actual fact this is the anteroom of the Rheinsfelden power station control centre, dated 1920.

Page 76
Wall anchors (left)
Wall surface crack (right)
Spinning mill, Neuthal spinning museum
Neuthal, Bäretswil, 1994
The old spinning mills still stand uncompromisingly in the landscape, and Neuthal is a particularly demonstrative example right across the valley. Nevertheless, it has been constantly changing during its long life, as shown by this wall surface crack and security anchors.

Page 77
"Chapel"
Brewery, BIWAG Uster
Uster, 1990
Before production processes were hidden away in covered shops, nearly everything was open to view. The open space under this chapel-like gabled roof was used for cooling freshly brewed beer.

Page 79
Firefighting water tank
Spinning mill, Neuthal spinning museum
Neuthal, Bäretswil, 1994
Ever since the first factories were built, fire protection has often been a matter of survival. Neuthal spinning mill, dating back to 1827, regarded buckets and this riveted water tank as adequate for the purpose.

Pages 80 and 81
Heating pipes
Refuse incineration plant, City of Basle
Basle, 1995
Large factories are a challenge to heating engineers, and Sulzer met this challenge by becoming specialists in industrial heating systems. These heating pipes in the staircase and canteen of Basle incineration plant date back to around 1940.

Page 82
Emergency exit
Spinning mill, STA Unteraathal
Aathal, 1989
Ever since the beginning of the industrial revolution, fire has left death and destruction in its wake again and again. Fire sprinklers and emergency exits have been compulsory in Swiss factories since 1890.

Page 83
Canteen
Spinning mill, STA Aathal
Aathal, 1990
A good many factories were a world of their own to the people who worked there. This was particularly true of the country spinning mills, whose canteens provided solid meals at low prices from home-grown produce.

Pages 84 and 85
Streiff collection
Spinning mill, Neuthal spinning museum
Neuthal, Bäretswil, 1994
Old junk? After being collected with loving care for decades, a lot of historical advertising material and equipment belonging to the textile and clothing industry had to be removed at short notice. Its rescue led to the founding of the Neuthal spinning museum.

Pages 86 and 87
Dinosaur exhibition
Spinning mill, now Siber + Siber dinosaur museum, Aathal
Aathal, 1993
Commercial reutilization is usually the only chance of survival for old factories. This rather eerie dinosaur museum in an Unteraathal spinning mill constitutes an exception.

Page 89
Control room
Pumped-water storage station, Ruppoldingen (ATEL)
Aarburg, 1991
Wherever old installations survive long enough, they often become valuable museum exhibits. Ruppoldingen pumped-water storage station, dating back to 1904, was the first of its kind in Switzerland.

Page 91
Entrance hall
Hydroelectric power station, City of Geneva
Geneva, 1992
Erected in 1886, Coulouvrenière drinking-water pumping station in Geneva was the largest hydroelectric installation in Switzerland. After dismantling 16 of the former 18 pump-turbines, this magnificent pumping station is now used for performances by the Geneva Opera.

Page 92
Fresh air intake
Spinning mill, STA Unteraathal
Aathal, 1991
Romantic ruins? After nearly 30 years of disuse, the damp walls of this 1851 spinning mill now harbour only the remains of the air-conditioning system added much later.

Page 93
Mezzanine floor
Hydroelectric power station, Eglisau (NOK)
Rheinsfelden, 1991
How much careful thought and design work must have gone into this project between 1915 and 1920? A double-glazed 3-sided window system at Eglisau power station.

Page 95
Fanlight window
Hydroelectric power station, City of Geneva
Geneva, 1992
Rather than technical functionality, classical elegance was the aim of this arched entrance to "la Coulouvrenière." Geneva was justly proud of its first comprehensive drinking-water supply system.

Page 97
Cable ducting
Hydroelectric power station, Mühleberg (BKW)
Mühleberg, 1991
Completed in 1921, Mühleberg power station on the Aare near Berne seems to have been devoted to concrete, inside and out—from cement facade to concrete cable ducting.

Page 98
Sprinklers
Spinning mill, STA Unteraathal
Aathal, 1989
In old factories only a few selected workers ever had access to the "catacombs"—such as these air humidification sprinklers, deep in the bowels of Unteraathal spinning mill.

Page 99
Staircase
Refuse incineration plant, City of Basle
Basle, 1995
These deceptively smooth railings led unsuspecting visitors down to a veritable Hades, where the king of the consumer industry underworld was appeased by unburnt sacrifices ranging from petfood tins to old flatirons.

Page 100
Intake gates
Hydroelectric power station, Eglisau (NOK)
Rheinsfelden, 1991
This intake gate had to stand up to thousands of tons of water pressure. It regulated water-flow from the Rhine to the turbines, according to power demand.

Page 101
Basement
Hydroelectric power station, Wägital (NOK)
Siebnen, 1992
Gigantic concrete structures transmit the inertia of the machinery above into the solid foundations below, leaving plenty of storage space between.

Page 103
Junction box
Lead mine, Goppenstein
Goppenstein, 1994
With ist insulation stripped and ist asbestos cover removed, this cast-in MHV junction box in its wooden case is no longer needed—since the last boom of 1952, the lead mine has fallen into ruins.

Page 104
Drainage pit
Hydroelectric power station, Mühleberg (NOK)
Mühleberg, 1991
70 years of rising and sinking water levels in this drainage pit with overflow pipe have left their traces on the carefully finished concrete.

Page 105
Tailrace
Spinning mill, STA Flos Wetzikon
Wetzikon, 1989
"Every drop of water shall flow through my mill!" Since waterpower was the only source of energy in those days, the Canton of Zurich developed one of Switzerland's densest ducting networks. The Aabach stream still flows under this old spinning mill.

Page 106
Vibratory shake-out machine in a foundry
Machine and metalworking industry, Sulzer Ltd
Oberwinterthur, 1991
During the course of time, the heaviest, unhealthiest and most dangerous tasks were slowly automated. The last substantial investment made by Sulzer at the Oberwinterthur foundry, closed down in 1993, was in vibratory shake-out machines.

Page 107
Exhaust stack
Refuse incineration plant, City of Basle
Basle, 1995
From the base of this chimney, which used to belch obnoxious flue gases into the atmosphere high above, a door opens into the refuse incineration kilns—the destruction machinery of consumer society.

Page 109
Charcoal mound
Charcoal plant, Alconchel
Alconchel, Spain, 1996
In the "good old days" long before our absurdly hectic age, the oak groves of Estremadura afforded a symbiotically Spartan living from the acorn harvest and pig-keeping, cork and charcoal production.

Page 114
Drive mechanism
Sawmill, Stockrüti
Stockrüti, Bäretswil, 1993
Stockrüti is the last surviving water-powered sawmill in the Zurich Uplands. The drive mechanism is an impressive combination of gearwheels, belts and pulleys.

Antispiece
Tools and implements
Metalworking and machine industry, Rolba AG
Wetzikon, 1990
Wire ropes, tow-ropes, hooks and tongs on a riveted tool rack in the Rolba erection bay—witnesses of former ski piste levelling-machine production.

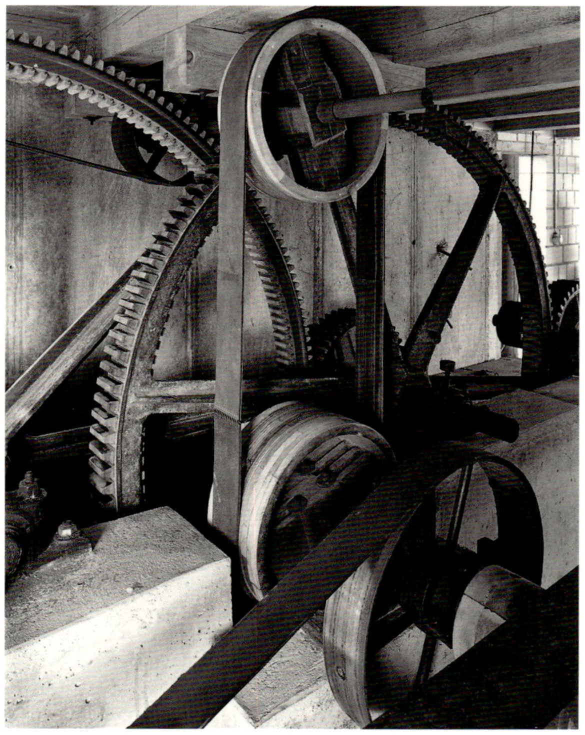

Epilogue

Ferit Kuyas

I have always interested myself in things which show the traces of their past—ruins, old barns, ancient tree trunks, cemeteries. This is very likely attributable to the interest of my parents in archaeology. It was quite natural, therefore, that as a photographer I would sooner or later hit upon industrial relics as a theme with archaeological associations.

Old factories have a peculiar fascination for me. Inside them I feel like an archaeologist searching for traces of a bygone civilization. And from 1987 to 1995 most of my time was taken up with this intensive search.

Originally on the lookout for what I thought would be good photographic subjects, I started to get more and more interested in creating expressive pictures which apart from mere documentation, would also have emotional appeal.

Today, I am convinced that during that period I was actually searching for my own identity. The years in which "Industrial Interiors" was composed mark a phase in my life when loneliness was my constant companion. Although influenced by a good many friends, that was largely a time of personal loss, insecurity and emptiness. In fact these pictures of industrial interiors can also be regarded as "personal interiors," reflecting to some extent my inner feelings during those years. But they also reflect the poetry, humor and aesthetics of life—which for me are a matter of survival.

In all my photographic work, I find the interplay of space, light and materials particularly important. Light makes materials come to life, and space without light is of no interest from the photographic point of view. Texture and surface characteristics—the essence of materials—form an ethereal link with industrial reality in these pictures. It is this which puts them on the borderline between documentation and pure emotion.

Hans-Peter Bärtschi

Hans-Peter Bärtschi, born in Zurich in 1950, has lived since 1957 in Winterthur (Switzerland). He studied architecture at the ETH Zurich, graduating with honors with a diploma project entitled "Reutilization of the Former Zurich Barracks-Site" with the architects Dolf Schneebli and Aldo Rossi. In 1979 he opened his Winterthur practice "ARIAS" for architecture, industrial archaeology and city development. His 520 page dissertation of 1980 on "Industrialization, Railways and City Construction" was published in Basle and Boston (USA). Of the 30 associations and groups to which he belongs, a dozen or so were founded due to his initiative—indeed, associations and societies have the greatest say in Switzerland when it comes to rescuing our industrial heritage from demolition. In the meantime, Hans-Peter Bärtschi's indefatigable efforts through his publications, exhibitions and field studies have long extended beyond the frontiers of the Canton of Zurich. He is a recognized authority on industrial archaeology not only in Switzerland, but also among international bodies. He still prefers, however, to work "on the job"—taking inventories and photographs, compiling archives, passing on his findings and vast knowledge to industrial culture enthusiasts, local authorities, companies and site owners alike.

Benedikt Loderer

Benedikt Loderer, born 1945 in Berne (Switzerland), was apprenticed as a draughtsman after leaving school. He then matriculated and studied architecture at the ETH Zurich, where he became an assistant professor. He also trained with Swiss television and worked for a firm of architects, finally taking up free-lance journalism for some years, during which he was architecture critic for the Zurich newspaper *Tages-Anzeiger*. In 1981 he completed his dissertation entitled "The Interior of Exteriors as the Exterior of Interiors." Between 1980 and 1986 he wrote three plays for radio and one for television, and was also part-time editor of the architectural journal *aktuelles bauen*. While working for Curti Medien AG publishers, he was responsible in 1988 for founding the architectural and design magazine *Hochparterre,* of which he became editor-in-chief. The publication of *Hochparterre* was taken over in the summer of 1991 by the editorial team, to which it has belonged ever since. In May 1997 he retired as editor-in-chief and became regular editor of *Hochparterre*, also contributing to other publications. Benedikt Loderer is thus an outstanding master of three arts: reading, writing and speaking. And that is his livelihood.

Ferit Kuyas

Biography

1955 Born in Istanbul, Turkey.
1961 Emigrates to Switzerland.
1971 Presented with his first camera by his father, an engineer and enthusiastic photographer.
1974 Architecture studies at the Federal Institute of Technology (ETH) in Zurich.
1977 Jurisprudence studies at Zurich University. Graduates in jurisprudence in 1982.
1983 Travels to San Diego, California. Starts intensive autodidactic study of photography. Color work in the reporting and natural photography fields.
1984 Starts photographing with his mother's old Rolleiflex 6x6.
1985 Edward Weston's picture "Dunes, Oceano" in the Stockeregg gallery, Zurich, deeply impresses him. Decides to concentrate henceforth on black and white photography.
1986 Attends Peter Gasser's workshop on black and white photography. Starts a landscape photography series named "Places—Orte" extending until 1988.
1987 Buys his first 4x5 inch camera, a Toyo 45A. Travels to Venice. Exchanges this camera during the summer for an 8x10 inch Toyo 810M, which he uses for most of his work during the next years. Discovers in winter the old Aathal valley factory buildings near Zurich.
1988 His comprehensive documentation of the old spinning mill buildings on the Aabach leads him to intensive photography of industrial themes.
1990 Meets the industrial archaeologist Hans-Peter Bärtschi, with whom a fruitful cooperation begins.
1991 Makes contact with the Nordostschweizerische Kraftwerke (NOK) power company, and starts photographing power stations. Gains Swiss nationality in the year of Switzerland's 700th anniversary. Travels regularly to Italy over the next few years.
1992 Meets the American photographer John Gossage. This meeting has a profound influence on his subsequent work. He purchases an arca-swiss 4x5 inch camera, and starts photographing in this format since he finds 8x10 inch technique too inflexible.
1994 Starts teaching photography at Brugg (Switzerland) vocational training school. Holds workshops on black and white photography. Creative work at this time focuses on the historical Goppenstein lead mine.
1995 First lecturing assignment for the Group of Autodidactic Photographers (GAF) Berne. Visits southern Spain. From now on creative work is mostly carried out while on his travels.
1996 Moves to a century-old factory building in Wädenswil near Zurich, where he has lived and worked ever since.
1997 Accepts an architectural teaching assignment at Aargau institute of higher education (Switzerland). Trips to China and Spain.
1998 Spends eight weeks in China working on a Shanghai photography project to be realized together with Edy Brunner and Marco Paoluzzo.

So o Exhibitions

1991 *Fabriken am Aabach,* Villa am Aabach, Uster, Switzerland
1993 *Brauerei Feldschlösschen,* Photogalerie Bild, Aarau, Switzerland
Industriekultur, Eisenwerk Frauenfeld, Switzerland
NOK (Nordostschweizerische Kraftwerke) headquarters, Baden, Switzerland
1994 *Der Industrielehrpfad Zürcher Oberland,* Textilmaschinenmuseum, Neuthal, Switzerland
Kulturzentrum Ziegelhütte, Appenzell, Switzerland
Die historische Bleimine Goppenstein, Lötschentaler Museum, Kippel, Switzerland
1995 *Fabrikwelten,* Stahlrain, Brugg, Switzerland
Industrielandschaften und Architekturfragmente, Alte Krone, Biel, Switzerland
1996 Mühlerama, Zurich
Innenwelten, steigerpartner, Zurich
1997 *Fabrikwelten,* Heimatwerk Bauma, Switzerland
1998 Villa am Aabach, Uster, Switzerland

G-oup Exhibitions

1987 Zentrum Roswiesen, Zurich
1988 Gemeinschaftszentrum Heerenschürli, Zurich
1991 Photogalerie Bild, Baden, Switzerland
1993 Gemeinschaftszentrum Heerenschürli, Zurich
1994 *Industriebild,* Fotomuseum Winterthur, Winterthur, Switzerland

Publications

1991 Ferit Kuyas, *Fabriken am Aabach* (Factories on the Aabach), portfolio of 45 photographs. Zurich: own edition.
1992 Ferit Kuyas et al. Calendar, joint publication with 11 Swiss-German photographers. Lugano: Ticino Vita.
Ferit Kuyas, *Die Brauerei* (The Brewery), sample book of 12 silver gelatine prints. Zurich: own edition.
1994 Hans-Peter Bärtschi and Ferit Kuyas, *Der Industrielehrpfad Zürcher Oberland* (On the Trail of Industrial History in the Zurich Uplands). Wetzikon: Druckerei Wetzikon.
Hans-Peter Bärtschi and Ferit Kuyas, "Kathedralen der Stromversorgung" (Cathedrals of Power Generation), in: *Sondernummer Energie* (special edition on energy), Pro Technorama, 3, Winterthur.
1995 Hans-Peter Bärtschi and Ferit Kuyas, "Ende Feuer nach 53 Jahren: Zur Geschichte der alten Basler Kehrichtverbrennungsanstalt, die zur Zeit abgerissen wird" (Cease-fire after 53 Years: a historical review of the old Basle refuse incineration plant), in: *Basler Magazin,* 42, Basel.
Max Matter, *Stelen am Stahlrain* (Pillars on the Stahlrain), Brugg.
Sylvia Bärtschi-Baumann, "Industriefotografie heute" (Industrial Photography Today), in: *IN.KU-Bulletin,* 17. Winterthur: Gesellschaft für Industriekultur (Association for Industrial Culture)
1996 *Dokumentation öffentlicher Bauten: Verkehrsleitzentrale Schafisheim* (Documentation of public buildings in the Canton of Aargau: Schafisheim traffic control centre). Aarau: Aarau Baudepartement des Kantons Aargau.
1997 *Dokumentation öffentlicher Bauten: Dienstleistungszentrum Zofingen* (Documentation of public buildings in the Canton of Aargau: Zofingen services centre). Aarau: Baudepartement des Kantons Aargau.

Acknowledgement

A work such as this is only possible together with a dedicated team. I sincerely thank all those who have participated in the production of this book and helped to further my professional development, in particular the following:

Aare-Tessin AG für Elektrizität, Aysegül and Peter Barbier, Hans-Peter Bärtschi, Susanne and Hans Bebié, Bernische Kraftwerke AG, BIWAG Getränke AG, Brauerei Feldschlösschen, Edy Brunner, Bündner Kraftwerke, Fotomuseum Winterthur, Freiburgische Elektrizitätswerke, Marc Funk, Peter Gasser, John Gossage, Kraftübertragungswerke Rheinfelden AG, Sabina and Kenneth C. Korfmann, Regula and Heinz Küng, Nihal and Tevfik Kuyas, Benedikt Loderer, Nordostschweizerische Kraftwerke, Marco Paoluzzo, Siber + Siber AG, Christina Sitte, Andi Streiff, Jakob Streiff and family, Spinnerei Streiff AG, Städtische Werke Basel, Sulzer Ltd Winterthur, Textilmaschinenmuseum Neuthal, Zellweger Uster.

This book has been supported by:

Nikon

BUNDESAMT FÜR KULTUR
OFFICE FEDERAL DE LA CULTURE
UFFICIO FEDERALE DELLA CULTURA
UFFIZI FEDERAL DA CULTURA
SWISS FEDERAL OFFICE OF CULTURE

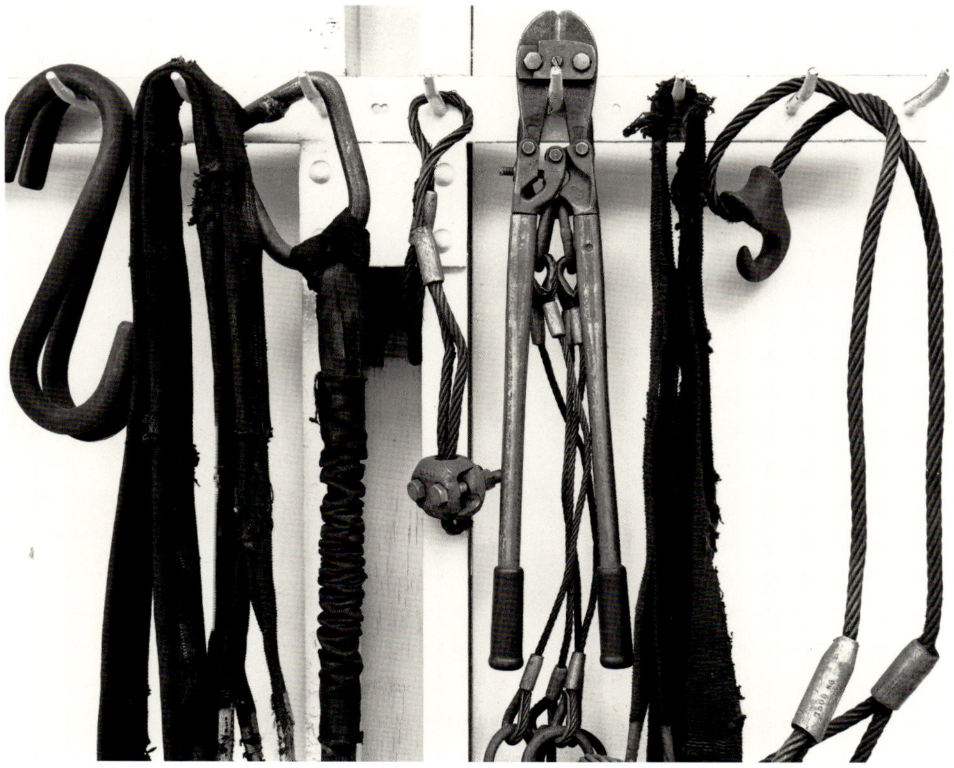

Captions by
Hans-Peter Bärtschi, ARIAS, Winterthur, Switzerland
Translation from the German by John P. Grimshaw, Zurich
Layout and Typography by
Christina Sitte, Donald Neuburger, Ferit Kuyas
Editorial direction by
Mirjam Ghisleni-Stemmle, Charlotte Staehelin
Photolithography and Typesetting by
Colorlith, Geroldswil—Zurich, Switzerland
Printed by
Offsetdruck Götz AG, Geroldswil—Zurich, Switzerland
Bound by
Buchbinderei Burkhardt AG, Mönchaltorf—Zurich,
Switzerland

ISBN 3-908161-78-9